FOUL DEEDS & SUSPICIOUS DEATHS
IN & AROUND BRISTOL

FOUL DEEDS AND SUSPICIOUS DEATHS Series

Wharncliffe's *Foul Deeds and Suspicious Deaths* series explores, in detail, crimes of passion, brutal murders and foul misdemeanours from early modern times to the present day. Victorian street crime, mysterious deaths and modern murders tell tales where passion, jealousy and social deprivation brought unexpected violence to those involved. From unexplained death and suicide to murder and manslaughter, the books provide a fascinating insight into the lives of both victims and perpetrators as well as society as a whole.

Other titles in the series include:

Foul Deeds and Suspicious Deaths in Bolton, Glynis Cooper
ISBN: 1-903425-63-8. £9.99

Foul Deeds and Suspicious Deaths in London's East End, Geoffrey Howse
ISBN: 1-903425-71-9. £10.99

Foul Deeds and Suspicious Deaths in London's West End, Geoffrey Howse
ISBN: 1-845630-01-7. £10.99

Foul Deeds and Suspicious Deaths in & Around Durham, Maureen Anderson
ISBN: 1-903425-46-8. £9.99

Foul Deeds and Suspicious Deaths in Hampstead, Holburn & St Pancras, Mark Aston
ISBN: 1-903425-94-8. £10.99

Foul Deeds and Suspicious Deaths in Colchester, Patrick Denney
ISBN: 1-903425-80-8. £10.99

Foul Deeds and Suspicious Deaths in Newport, Terry Underwood
ISBN: 1-903425-59-X. £9.99

Foul Deeds and Suspicious Deaths Around Derby, Kevin Turton
ISBN: 1-903425-76-X. £9.99

Foul Deeds and Suspicious Deaths in and Around Scunthorpe, Stephen Wade
ISBN: 1-903425-88-3. £9.99

More Foul Deeds and Suspicious Deaths in Wakefield, Kate Taylor
ISBN: 1-903425-48-4. £9.99

Foul Deeds and Suspicious Deaths in York, Keith Henson
ISBN: 1-903425-33-6. £9.99

Foul Deeds and Suspicious Deaths on the Yorkshire Coast, Alan Whitworth
ISBN: 1-903425-01-8. £9.99

Foul Deeds and Suspicious Deaths in Coventry, David McGrory
ISBN: 1-903425-57-3. £9.99

Foul Deeds and Suspicious Deaths in Manchester, Martin Baggoley
ISBN: 1-903425-65-4. £9.99

Foul Deeds and Suspicious Deaths in Newcastle, Maureen Anderson
ISBN: 1-903425-34-4. £9.99

Foul Deeds and Suspicious Deaths in Hull, David Goodman
ISBN: 1-903425-43-3. £9.99

Foul Deeds and Suspicious Deaths Around Newport, Terry Underwood
ISBN: 1-903425-59-X. £9.99

Please contact us via any of the methods below for more information or a catalogue.
WHARNCLIFFE BOOKS
47 Church Street – Barnsley – South Yorkshire S70 2AS
Tel: 01226 734555 – 734222; Fax: 01226 724438
E-mail: enquiries@pen-and-sword.co.uk
Website: www.wharncliffebooks.co.uk

Foul Deeds & Suspicious Deaths In & Around

BRISTOL

VERONICA SMITH

Series Editor
Brian Elliott

Wharncliffe Books

Publisher's note: Veronica Smith died soon after completing this book.

First Published in Great Britain in 2006 by
Wharncliffe Books
an imprint of
Pen and Sword Books Ltd
47 Church Street
Barnsley
South Yorkshire
S70 2AS

ISBN: 1 845630 13 0

Typeset in 11/13pt Plantin by Concept, Huddersfield.

Printed and bound in England by CPI UK

Pen and Sword Books Ltd incorporates the Imprints of
Pen & Sword Aviation, Pen & Sword Maritime,
Pen & Sword Military, Wharncliffe Books,
Pen & Sword Select, Pen and Sword Military Classics
and Leo Cooper.

For a complete list of Pen & Sword titles please contact
PEN & SWORD BOOKS LIMITED
47 Church Street
Barnsley
South Yorkshire
S70 2AS
England
E-mail: enquiries@pen-and-sword.co.uk
Website: www.pen-and-sword.co.uk

Contents

Dedication

I would like to dedicate this book to the doctors and nursing staff at the Bristol Royal Infirmary, especially my recently retired consultant Dr Richard Mountford; also the current team which comprises Dr Chris Probert, Dr Tom Creed, Dr Tanvir Ahmed and Raveen Kandan. Due a special mention, too, are Aileen Fraser and Lynne Williams and the nurses on Wards 14 and 11. Included also are all those at St Michael's who have done so much for me: Mr John Murdoch, Dr Jo Bailey and Sister Hilary Reynolds and her wonderful staff on Ward 78. Thanks, too, to Dr Chris Williams, my Oncologist and to the support team past and present: Helen Jones, Jenny James, Katy Horton-Fawkes and Yvonne Higgins who have never failed to raise my spirits when the going got tough.

Acknowledgements

My thanks go to George Elliott who was able to provide me with so much information on the Hanham Woods murder ('Murder on a May Morning') as well as sharing the results of his research with me. Thanks, too, are owed to Olive Jarrett for first-hand information regarding the same case.

I am immensely grateful to the staff at the Bristol Central Library for their endless patience in dealing with my queries and particularly to Dawn Dyer for solving the final outcome of the Ferris case ('Bloodshed on her Birthday') at the eleventh hour.

A debt of gratitude, also, to Kevin and Christine Webb of the *Dundry Inn* for making me so welcome and furthering my knowledge of the area and to Gaynor and Steve Wedmore for persuading me to research 'A Dastardly Deed at Dundry'.

It was interesting to discover my life-long friends, the Hoptons, were related to victim and slayer in 'A Ferocious Fratricide' and, to meet by chance Brenda Joy another member of the clan. I should like to thank Richard Webber and Denis Wright for information relating to Russell's Fields ('Charlotte's Concealment'). Others who have provided me with personal knowledge of the cases within this book are Denis Rugman ('The Riddle of Richard Rugman'), Vi Allen ('Evil in Easton'), Mrs Joyce Davies ('Decoyed to his Death') and Mike Hooper ('What Lies Beneath'). Thanks also to Jonathan Rowe for additional information relating to the same case.

Lastly, my sincere thanks to Richard Burley at the Bristol Records Office for his initial recommendation to my publishers.

Introduction

I am sure there are many who consider me of an extremely bloodthirsty nature because of my interest in writing about old murders but they would be totally wrong. I actually abhor violence and could never imagine myself being able to defend myself even were I placed in a dangerous situation. I certainly am quite convinced that I could never injure anyone, let alone kill someone. Why then am I fascinated by other people's crimes?

Well, I am fascinated by everything other people do. I have lived my life fairly passively, more of a watcher than a woman of action. I am intrigued by the motivation of others; their passions; their towering rages; their obsessions – all emotions completely outside my experience. I yearn only for a calm, restful, pain-free life but it is interesting to see how other folk react to certain situations.

Many of the cases I have chosen to research take place a century or so ago. Social history is an exciting subject to me and the reports contained in bygone newspapers give such a wealth of detail making it a relatively simple matter to reconstruct life as it must have been for the participants in some of the dramas that unfolded in the little back streets of Bristol and the wilds of the surrounding countryside many decades ago.

Bristol itself is an impressive city and fortunately one whose history has been well-documented. There exist sketches and photographs of areas which disappeared many years back enabling a clear insight of the conditions under which different generations lived, loved and, occasionally, killed.

A pattern emerges if we study murder throughout history. Perhaps up until the seventeenth century slayings were frequently politically motivated or arose from religious differences. No doubt private poisonings took place but guilt would have been hard to prove in the days before food hygiene became an issue and accidents could easily be arranged in dimly-lit dwellings with winding steep staircases and slippery stone steps.

The author – Veronica Smith

Money has always provided strong motivation for murder but, in the main, the cases I have studied have been desperate people looking for solutions to seemingly insoluble problems. Young girls finding themselves pregnant, penniless and lacking the protection of a husband; enraged husbands finding their slattern wives have spent the rent money on booze; and love triangles where feelings of loss and rejection were too much to bear. These were situations which drove some to kill.

And there are some slayings which remain a mystery. Undoubtedly there are those who do, indeed, get away with murder. It is sometimes an uncomfortable thought that the person behind you in the queue at the check out, or that one sitting by you on the bus could ... maybe ... but, surely not? Such an ordinary-looking person. But murderers generally are ...

CHAPTER 1

A Ferocious Fratricide
1741

The whole case caused
an absolute sensation ...

There is a horror and brutality surrounding the Goodere case that seems to echo down the centuries, rendering it every bit as perturbing now as it must have been then. The affair was one that caught the imagination of Bristol surgeon Richard Smith for whom the macabre in general held a fascination. His interest is a fortunate one for researchers as he compiled a scrapbook in the early years of the nineteenth century in which many local crimes are precisely detailed.

Another interesting aspect of the case is that members of the Goodere family (who now spell it Goodyer) are still resident in the Bristol area. Papers passed down from earlier generations speak of the family's descent from the Kings of Wessex, this being the reason they were permitted a heraldic crest of a wyvern rampant.

The murder was committed on 19 January 1741, the result of simmering hatred harboured against Sir John Dineley, Bart, by his brother, Samuel Goodere, a loathing that had festered for many years.

Sir John had dropped the last part of his name, 'Goodere', on succeeding to a maternal estate in Worcestershire and had married the grand-daughter and heiress of Alderman John Lawford thus taking into his possession two mansions, one at Stapleton and another at Tockington, near Thornbury. It is said that Sir John behaved in an irrational and almost insane manner and took advantage of a loophole in the entail of the family estates to will all properties to his nephews, two young men by the name of Foote. Thus he effectively impoverished the former heir presumptive, Samuel Goodere who understandably felt extremely bitter. In October 1740 he was appointed to the command of the *Ruby* after the previous captain had committed suicide. It was around this time he vowed to kill his brother and began to work out a plan to carry out his intent. He approached Mr Jarritt Smith, a solicitor with whom he knew his brother had dealings, and urged him to endeavour to bring about a reconciliation, saying that Mr Smith's house on College Green might be a suitable venue for the meeting. The solicitor agreed and persuaded Sir John to attend such a meeting on his next visit to Bristol. The first available date was 13 January and this news was conveyed to Captain Goodere's lodgings in Prince's Street.

Captain Goodere immediately rallied some sailors from the *Ruby* and hired further ruffians who were serving on the *Vernon* privateer and gave them orders to seize Sir John when he left the solicitor's house, the site of which is where the *Swallow Hotel* stands today. Sir John kept his appointment with his

College Green in the eighteenth century. From a painting by Samuel Scott. Bristol Museum and Art Gallery

College Green – the scene today. The author

attorney because he was negotiating a mortgage for £5,000 to clear some debts but declined to see his brother on this occasion. Added to the fact that Sir John and his servant were well-mounted and fully armed, it was decided to delay the attack until Sir John's next visit scheduled for Sunday, 19 January.

The captain then proceeded to make the necessary arrangements. Almost opposite Mr Smith's house was the *White Hart* alehouse. A room on the first floor projected over the porch giving a clear view of traffic passing to and from the quays. Goodere installed his assassins in the room on the Sunday afternoon while he made his way to the meeting at Mr Jarritt Smith's. Once there he greeted his estranged brother warmly, kissed him and remarked that he appeared to be in better health. Wine was poured and Mr Smith called for a toast to

The White Hart *on College Green where Goodere's men lay in wait for Sir John Dineley. From Richard Smith's scrapbook.* Bristol Records Office

'love and friendship' to which Sir John responded 'With all my heart'. The captain raised his glass and drank and the solicitor believed the reconciliation to be complete. He bade his guests goodbye at his front door and saw Sir John walk towards the quay while the captain was soon surrounded by sailors spilling out of the alehouse. He was heard to say 'Is he ready?' adding an order to 'make haste'. Mr Smith assumed Goodere to be giving instructions regarding his vessel to his men, thought no more of the matter and closed his door.

A few seconds later Matthew Mahoney, the leader of Goodere's men, seized Sir John as he passed under the wall of St Augustine's churchyard and, with the help of his confederates, partly carried and partly dragged his captive along Captain Day's ropewalk towards the *Ruby*'s barge which was moored near Mardyke. Captain Goodere brought up the rear fending off questions from curious bystanders by explaining that the prisoner was a murderer who was being taken on board ship to face trial. Brutality was commonplace down on the quays where the press gangs operated so that when one of Goodere's men threatened to throw one enquirer into the river the group were left to their own devices in spite of their prisoner crying out several times 'Murder! I am Sir John Dineley'. His red cloak was rapidly thrown over his head and he was hustled aboard the barge which was then rowed to Kingroad. The captain had taken the precaution of warning his crew that his brother was mad. Later, Samuel Goodere was to say that his brother began to remonstrate with him, asking why he was being used so, and that his 'heart relented a little but I thought I had gone too far to retract or curb my fixed resolution'.

Before going for his supper, Goodere instructed Weller, the carpenter, to fix two strong bolts on the outside of the door. Sir John was complaining about all manner of aches and pains so the captain had the doctor examine him. He was told his brother's pulse was normal. Sir John refused a glass of rum. After supper the captain visited his brother once more on the pretext of taking him in some clean stockings but the mission was really to ascertain his position in the cabin and decide the best way to carry out the evil deed.

Between two and three the following morning the captain instructed Mahoney to call up Charles White, another crew member. Elisha Cole was supposed to be assisting Mahoney but he had drunk too much rum and was out cold. White was ushered into the cabin and offered a quart of rum. When this had taken effect he was asked if he was prepared to kill a Spaniard. The man looked more than a little surprised but the other two men were able to convince him it was his duty to his country. By this time Matthew Mahoney was having doubts and was extremely reluctant to take part in the murder but Goodere told him he had agreed and now he had to go through with it. He handed Mahoney a handkerchief and a piece of half-inch rope. The idea was to strangle Sir John with the rope and stuff the handkerchief into his mouth to prevent him shouting out. Upon reaching the cabin door Goodere ordered the sentry to hand over his sword. The sentry came forward to offer a candle to light the captain's way but Goodere ordered him off. He entered the cabin to see his brother take his last breath and gasp 'Oh my poor life!'. The captain confirmed with Mahoney and White that his brother was, indeed, dead so he locked the cabin and took his two men into his own cabin. Mahoney handed over the dead man's gold watch to Goodere and received a silver one in return and the men were paid off, each being given over £14 although White had a little more cash as Mahoney had been given the watch.

The plan was that the body should be sewn into a hammock and thrown overboard or, if the body was discovered earlier, it would be passed off as a suicide by strangulation.

In the event all this elaborate planning was in vain. Other crew members had watched much of the action through chinks in the woodwork and the following morning, after Mahoney and White had taken themselves off to the city, and Goodere, presumably, was resting after all his exertion, the cooper and the carpenter broke into the cabin and, with the help of eight or ten crew members they arrested the captain and sent for the water bailiff. Later, Mahoney and White were apprehended in the city. Captain Goodere denied his guilt and alleged that his brother was insane but, by this time, Samuel himself was acting rather strangely. He forwarded a petition to the Crown protesting his innocence and insisted on wearing a red cloak, the badge of the upper classes, when he was marched through the streets to Newgate. He attempted to hire a gang of colliers to rescue him from his place of execution. One of his sons was later to die in a lunatic asylum.

The whole case caused an absolute sensation in the city and poems, plays and pamphlets were published relating to all the gory details. All three men were hanged on the gallows which stood upon St Brevel's stone, on St Michael's Hill, on 17 April 1741.

A fourth murderer was also hanged that day, an Irishwoman called Jane Williams from Marsh Street who had drowned her infant child. After the execution her many friends and neigh-

Wine Street. Mahoney and White sought out the taverns here after the deed was done. Arrowsmith's Directory of Bristol, 1898

bours carried off her body 'keeping up a howl all the way to the Quay'. When they arrived there they opened up the shell in which the body had been placed and placed it on a bench at the corner of Old Nick's Entry and collected coins from passers by to pay for a decent funeral, a mass and a wake (apparently Old Nick's Entry was not a reference to the devil but was so called because a man called Nicholson kept an ale house there where Bristol *Home Brewed* was served).

The bodies of Matthew Mahoney and Charles White were borne away to be hung in chains while the body of Captain Samuel Goodere was taken to the infirmary to be dissected. Afterwards his remains were returned to his friends who took them back to his parish church in Gloucestershire. Mahoney was gibbeted on Dunball Island in a place known as 'The Swatch'.

The story has a strange footnote, of particular interest to the ghoulish surgeon, Richard Smith. In 1841 he was contacted by a man called Richard Rowlands living on Broad Quay, whose brother, Samuel, had something he thought might be of interest to Mr Smith. Curiously, Samuel kept the liquor shop next to the *Steam Packet* hotel in Old Nick's Entry where Jane Williams' pals had tried to raise money for her funeral. Samuel explained that the irons had been brought back to shore by a couple of fellows aboard the *Jupiter* privateer who had been stranded there one time when the tide turned. Then, more recently, the gibbet itself had collapsed and had been brought off The Swatch by a man called Browne, a Pill pilot. It was then sold to a firm at Crockerne, Pill, where it was saved from being cut up. Richard Smith, needless to say, acquired both gibbet and chains to be placed in the infirmary museum. A tiny segment of this grim relic remains in his scrap book which is now housed in the Bristol Records Office. Somehow the sight of it seems to highlight the horror of the entire episode.

CHAPTER 2

Bloodshed on Her Birthday
1846

There were pools of blood in the house and on the pavement outside.

Sunday 1 November 1846 was Louisa Ferris's twenty-ninth birthday. It is doubtful we shall ever know how the day began but the ending guaranteed that life for her family would never be the same again.

Louisa, a small, dainty, rather pale woman, with light auburn hair, had married at 16 and had given birth to three children, one of whom had died before the dreadful events in November 1846. She and her husband, who worked as a carrier, had separated the previous year after long-standing domestic disagreements – none, apparently, precipitated by any wrongdoing on the part of Louisa. Her husband had gone to live near Chepstow. It was rumoured he owned property there.

Louisa continued to live in the Lawrence Hill area but her mother who was married to a police sergeant at Trinity Road police station and was, in fact, the housekeeper there, had concerns regarding her daughter's financial security so a house was found for her in Lion Street, Easton where there were enough rooms for her to have lodgers thus bolstering her income.

The house comprised two bedrooms, a front and back parlour and a kitchen. There were, it seems, four lodgers in the house, William Stone, William Ferris, Elizabeth Jones and

An old map of Easton showing Lawrence Hill and Lion Street (marked with an asterisk). Arrowsmith's Directory of Bristol, 1898

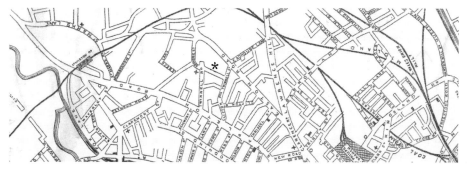

Lion Street pictured in the 1960s shortly before demolition. Bristol Evening Post

Patrick White, a policeman who had lodged at her previous address. Might he, perhaps, have been recommended by Louisa's stepfather, Sergeant Franklyn?

The *Bristol Mercury* announced, after reporting the subsequent inquest, that there 'are circumstances in the history' and 'particularly in relation to her connexion with White' which made Louisa 'to some extent, an object of commiseration'. It was said that he had been acquainted with her for a long time and had made 'overtures of an improper nature which she more than once rejected'. He, apparently, 'accomplished her ruin by means of drugged liqueurs' – clearly a forerunner of Rohypnol. The affair continued (with or without the doctored drinks is not specified) and soon the inevitable happened, Louisa became pregnant. Rather than risk the scandal the smooth-tongued Irishman persuaded her to procure an abortion.

This, then, was the background to the tragedy which was to unfold on that Sunday afternoon.

Louisa's brother, James Edwards, decided to pay her a visit. She had been pestering him for ages to come and see her so what made him decide to call in on that fateful day is anybody's guess. It was not that he lived a great distance away for he gave his address as 3 Hookey's Court, Rosemary Street from whence he could have walked at a brisk pace in 20 minutes. In point of fact, though, he would not have needed to walk as he was a fly-driver (a fly being a lightweight, two-wheeled, horse-drawn vehicle). It was in this that he arrived that afternoon with a young friend called Charles Sainsbury. Charles lived with his father, a publican, in Prince Street. James had met Charles by chance that day on the Wells Road after dropping off a fare in Knowle. Charles, who was 18, wanted to visit a pal in 'Thistle Street' by which he must have meant Thrissell Street. James gave him a lift there but the friend proved elusive so he was persuaded to accompany Jim to his sister's new residence. When they knocked on the door they could get no reply but a neighbour called out that the children were round the back playing in the garden. Jim left Charles by the front door, swiftly returning and the door was then opened by Louisa Ferris who invited them to step into the house. It is at this juncture that memories of the witnesses began to conflict.

Charles Sainsbury stated that they had arrived at Lion Street at about 4 o'clock and that his friend's sister was in the downstairs back room. At that time the only people present were himself, James Edwards, Mrs Ferris and a young woman. They all sat down and about a couple of minutes later the policeman came downstairs and sat in an armchair by the fireplace with his back to the window. He sent the young woman out for a quart of beer and they all had a drink. He noted that Mrs Ferris had no conversation with the policeman but confined her remarks to her brother. They were discussing family matters. Charles talked with the policeman. He said at this time the policeman wore no coat, waistcoat or neckerchief and his braces were 'hanging down behind him'. He wore no shoes but fetched himself some slippers to put on.

After about an hour, according to Charles, Mrs Ferris went into the back-kitchen then swiftly returned to stand behind White, her right arm round his right shoulder as though she was

The Lion *public house. Was this where Elizabeth Jones was sent to fetch the beer?*
The author

whispering to him. Charles meanwhile was deep in conversation with Jim. He became aware of a groaning sound and saw
the policeman rise from the chair and take a few steps forward.
He realised White was bleeding and heard Jim say 'Louisa, my
God, what have you done?'. Louisa moved her chair a little way
back towards the kitchen and sat down again. It was getting
dark by this time and no candles had been lit nor was there a fire
in the grate. Charles admitted he was frightened and made his
exit through the back door. On his way he stopped at the police
station and saw Mrs Ferris arrive there in the fly. He heard her
direct her brother to stop by the station house.

When Jim was called to give evidence at the inquest which
was held at the *New Inn*, Lawford's Gate. He stated that he
had never, to the best of his knowledge, met White before that

afternoon. He either knew little of her personal circumstances or preferred not to commit himself, saying that he had no idea of her financial situation and that he believed her husband was living but thought they had been separated for about a year. When his sister came to the door, he said, her appearance 'indicated that she had just got up and had been drinking'. They all sat down in the back room where a young woman was present and shortly afterwards the policeman joined them partially dressed as previously described by Charles Sainsbury. They all drank some rum and then the young woman fetched in some beer. After this she left the room. At some stage one of the children joined them, a little girl. About 20 minutes after the young woman had gone out of the room the policeman disappeared followed, within a few minutes, by his sister. 'She very soon returned,' he said, 'in a dreadful state of mind, saying "Oh that wretch! Is this your promise? They are both upstairs on the bed".' She again left the room and, within a short while, White returned and sat back in his chair by the fireplace. Louisa re-entered the back parlour, still exclaiming 'Ah, you wretch, you nasty wretch! Is this your promise?'. As Jim leaned forward to pour out a glass of beer for White his sister rushed behind him. As he leaned forward to pass White the glass he saw his sister's hand moving from the man's throat in a very swift movement and then she quickly left the room. Sainsbury took fright and rushed out of the back door and Jim was left trying to help White who was bleeding badly. White shook off Jim and crawled on his hands and knees into the street, the front door being open. Neighbours were gathering round by this time so when his sister appeared from the back entrance to the house begging him to take her to the station house Jim felt that there were enough people on hand to look after the injured man so he helped Louisa into the vehicle and drove her to the requested destination. After she had surrended herself he went in to inform their mother of what had occurred.

It was then the young woman's turn to tell her tale. She gave her name as Elizabeth Jones, said she was unmarried and lodged at 12 Lion Street. She had a mother, Sarah, living at Calne who was married to a man called John Orchard. Elizabeth admitted that between four and five on the Sunday she was at home but heard no quarrel between the policeman and Mrs Ferris. She said that she had opened the door to the two young men and, at the time, Mrs Ferris and White were sitting in the back parlour. As soon as the men arrived she took herself off to bed. She explained that she had fetched two quarts of beer, at 6d a quart, at 1.30 which she, White and Mrs Ferris had drunk between them and she had gone out to buy another quart at 3.30. Mr White and Mrs Ferris had been playing dominoes and White had won the beer from her. She said that White had drunk very little but had forced the beer on Mrs Ferris and herself which is why she took herself off to bed. She awoke to find White standing by her bed and Mrs Ferris in the doorway. Shortly afterwards White followed Mrs Ferris from the room. When Elizabeth came downstairs Mrs Ferris accosted her and said she 'had a mind to serve her in the same fashion'. Elizabeth rushed out of the house encountering White as she did so. He was crawling on his hands and knees. She took refuge in the house next door. When she calmed down she noticed there was blood on her neck but she had no idea how it came to be there. Answering questions put by the coroner, she said she had not been aware of any razors being in the house and stated that they usually sat in the back parlour. She left her room after Mrs Ferris and Patrick White had gone downstairs. She heard a noise down there.

Louisa Ferris had elected to remain in court and hear all the evidence. It was reported that 'she appeared in the deepest affliction and cried bitterly, every now and again wringing her hands in evident agony or burying her face as if anxious to shut out all external objects'. During the course of the proceedings she was given permission to retire.

The jury, described by the *Bristol Mercury* as 'highly respectable' were taken to Lion Street to view the body which lay on a bed in the front parlour of 12 Lion Street. It presented a 'shocking spectacle', with the windpipe completely severed and the man's clothing saturated with blood. There were pools of blood in the house and on the pavement outside.

Inspector Henry Phillips Webb deposed that he knew the deceased who had served with the Bristol force for more than 7 years. He believed the man to be about 33 years of age, an

Irishman and unmarried. He knew that he had lodged with Mrs Ferris for the past 6 weeks, firstly at Lawrence Hill then in Lion Street. It was Inspector Webb whom Louisa had first encountered on entering the station crying 'Oh Mr Webb, you must take me into custody!'. When he asked her why she replied 'I have cut a man's throat!' The inspector soon realised that 'she was affected by drink'. At that point Sergeant Franklyn came to the charge room door and asked his step-daughter what the matter was and she 'raved out, as a person in hysterics would rave', saying 'That man has disgraced me – and you'.

That day and the next members of the public who were in Lion Street that Sunday afternoon were cross-examined. Robert Coombs who was a brick-burner by trade and lived at number 14 recalled Jim Edwards and his friend arriving in the fly at about 3 o'clock because they asked directions to Louisa Ferris's house. He saw the fly stop outside for about 30 minutes then disappear, returning in about 10 minutes and the driver going round to the back of the house. There was no sign of his companion. The next thing he noticed was the rattling of the carriage door at about 4.30 or 5 o'clock when he heard the flyman say 'Oh dear, he's a dead man'. Coombs, who lived next door but one, looked round and saw White crawling along the pavement. He heard the injured man muttering as he hurried towards him. By the time he reached the man a Mr Griffiths was with him, wiping the blood from his throat with a handkerchief, holding his hand against the wound in an attempt to stop the flow of blood. White was heard to say 'Mrs Ferris has cut my throat with a razor, pray for me,' to which Mr Griffiths rather tartly replied 'Pray yourself, my good fellow'. White then said 'Lord have mercy on my soul' and repeated it twice more, each time more faintly. He was failing fast and someone fetched a pillow to place under his head.

Richard Griffiths, a cabinet-maker from Redcliff Street, was visiting Lion Street that afternoon, arriving at 3.30. An hour or so later he noticed a young woman pass the window 'apparently tipsy with her hair about her neck'. He heard a strange noise and went to investigate. He was confronted with the sight of White crawling along the pavement. Griffiths thought at first the man was drunk, then he saw the blood and endeavoured to assist. He instructed someone to go for a doctor for, by this time, the neighbours were in the street wondering what was happening.

At number 11 lived John Llewellin, a cooper. He lived directly opposite Mrs Ferris's house but did not know her even by sight. Neither did he know the victim. Alerted by noises in the street he, too, had gone out to see what was going on. His lodger, Isaac Hawker, followed suit. They noticed the fly parked outside the house opposite and then it being driven off at speed. They then saw the injured man begin to crawl across the street. Someone said 'His throat is cut' and Llewellin tore off the canvas apron he was wearing and they bound it round the man's throat enabling him to say a few words but he was weakening by the second and expired before the arrival of the doctor.

Police Constable Robert Kingston was patrolling Easton Road at about 4.45 when someone approached him and said a man had had his throat cut in Lion Street. He hurried to the spot, recognized White and spoke to him but by this time the man was close to death and made no reply. Kingston then, aided by some of the neighbours, searched the house and remained on duty there until 2.00 am on the Monday morning. The body of Patrick White was carried into the house and placed on a bed in the front parlour.

The police surgeon, Charles Hanson, who had known Patrick White, then gave his deposition and carefully described the fatal wound which was made by a sharp instrument, such as a razor, just one gash from right to left which had completely severed the windpipe. He said that the deceased had signs of disease of the liver from the use of spirits and 'had all the appearances of a person addicted to drink' but his death was due entirely to the wound to the jugular vein and the artery, partly through loss of blood but also through the flow of blood into the bronchial tubes by way of the divided windpipe causing suffocation. It was the type of injury which could have been caused by a man intent on suicide but he had never seen a self-inflicted wound so deep. He did not think the man's life could have been saved even if a surgeon had been present.

Because of conflicting evidence the coroner recalled both Sainsbury and Edwards but, even so, some aspects of events were not fully explained. At last Louisa Ferris herself was called back into the court and advised she stood charged with cutting the throat of Patrick White and that the jury were about to retire to debate whether her crime had been that of murder or manslaughter. She was asked if she had any explanation to make regarding her actions but she replied, in a low tone 'I have nothing to say'. She then was given the option of being removed from the court which she took while the coroner summed up the evidence and then the jury were called upon to give their verdict which, after a short deliberation, was one of wilful murder whereupon she was committed upon the coroner's warrant to take her trial for that offence. In the event that trial did not take place until the following April and then the venue was Gloucester. This was perhaps because of the sensitivity of the case involving, as it did, a police officer.

The same evidence was presented as had been at the inquest with a few slight variations in statements. Mr Keating, who represented Mrs Ferris made a plea to the jury to bring in a verdict of manslaughter and, after 10 minutes discussion, that was the decision they reached. As she stood to receive sentence the judge spoke to her as follows:

You have had a very narrow escape; you have been found guilty of killing a person with whom you had been living in adultery. It shows the dreadful course of vice leading from one crime to another. It is necessary to make a severe example of you; human life has been sacrificed, probably without premeditation on your part, and no doubt causing you much regret. You have given way to a dreadful passion – you have sent him, without time for repentance to answer for his crimes, before his Maker. You will have time, and probably a long time, by the mercy of the jury, for repentance; but you must repent in a foreign land, never more to return.

At this juncture Louisa cried out 'do not banish me, my Lord, from my poor children!'. Her pleas, though, were in vain and the sentence of transportation for life stood.

Louisa Ferris was sent to Van Diemen's Land and, it was later reported in Felix Farley's *Bristol Journal* that she 'behaved herself in a most exemplary manner' and was granted a ticket of leave. It would be a true happy ending if it could be said she sailed for England to be reunited with her children but, sadly, this was not to be for almost immediately afterwards she cut another man's throat in Melbourne and was waiting execution for the deed when the newspaper went to print in September 1852.

CHAPTER 3

The Barbaric Butcher
1846

The dear child is dead ...
the dear child is dead.

t the same Gloucester Assize sessions as Louisa Ferris received her sentence another Bristolian was facing trial for an appalling crime. John Cann was 20 years old, married and the father of a 10-week-old baby girl called Anne Elizabeth. He was a resident of Campbell Terrace, Baptist Mills, 5 feet 6 inches tall with black hair and hazel eyes, he had a round face with a fresh complexion and there was a scar on his left cheek.

He is described as being a butcher and later evidence seems to suggest he ran his own shop but studying trade directories

The Warwick Arms, *Baptist Mills.* John Merrett collection

The Berkley Arms, *Baptist Street which led to Campbell Terrace where John and Elizabeth Cann lived.* John Merrett collection

for that period of Bristol's history it would seem to be that he came from a family of butchers. The shop at 70 Redcliffe Street was for many years in the ownership of a John Cann but it can almost certainly be assumed that this was his father's shop, which he may have managed on his father's behalf. It was later to emerge that, prior to his marriage, he lived with his father in what was entered into Gloucester Prison records as 'Rackcliffe

Redcliffe Street where John Cann ran his butcher's shop. John Merrett collection

Street' at which time he attended 'Rackcliffe church' but this mistake could well be blamed on his accent. Even today the pronunciation sometimes emerges as 'Reckliffe'. In All Saints' Row, at the back of St Nicholas Market was another butcher's shop, this one owned by a Mary Cann who may have been a sister or aunt.

The incident which was to alter the course of Cann's life forever took place on a December night in 1846. On the morning of 7 December Cann was drinking at a pub called the *Sugar Loaf*, probably the one in Nicholas Street. Perhaps he had been attending to business in Mary's shop. He was in the company of Thomas Williams who was later to say he remembered Cann's wife, Elizabeth, coming in with the baby in her arms between 10 and 11 o'clock. Cann held the child for a while saying he wished it had been a boy. Between 12 noon and 1 o'clock the party adjourned to the *Queen's Head*. This may have been the

The view from Back of Bridge Street where the atrocity was committed. Lewis Wilshire collection

one in St James' Barton. There Williams treated the party, which had increased to five, to '3 half-pints of rum and shrub.' 'Shrub' was composed of lime or lemon juice and sugar and was commonly drunk with rum, although any spirit could be used. The name derives from the Arabic *shurb* from which the words syrup and shebert also originate. The group had already sunk 4 or 5 quarts of 'Burton' which was a bitter beer, a typical working man's drink.

During their time in the *Queen's Head* Cann, apparently, 'took the child from his wife, nursed it, and held it up towards the gas'. Whether this indicates there was gas lighting at the inn is unclear. A number of the streets in the city were certainly gas-lit by 1846.

After this session Thomas Williams took himself home. Not so John Cann who was next spotted in Bath Street by John Thomas Lee, a policeman who had known him for some 7 or

8 years. Shortly afterwards he heard a woman screaming on the other side of the river, the thoroughfare known then as Back of Bridge Street, now the pathway bordering Castle Park. Lee swiftly made his way there and was in time to see Cann knock his wife down and then kick her. The wife was crying 'Murder!' then said 'The dear child is dead ... the dear child is dead'. As Lee approached he saw Mrs Cann was trying to drag the baby from the ground by its clothes. The policeman picked up the child and saw it was, indeed, dying and told Cann 'It is dying as far as it can', to which Cann replied 'It cannot die but once'. Mrs Cann said that her husband had kicked the baby in the head and thrown it across the road three times. She also said that he had sworn that very morning that he would 'get some sleeping stuff which would put it to sleep so that it should never wake up again and now he has done it'.

John Cann was taken into custody in the early hours of the morning of 8 December. He appeared very matter-of-fact about the whole affair, enquiring of William Harris, the custody officer, what time he would be taken before the magistrates and asking what Harris considered his fate would be. He said they could have done nothing to him if he had told his wife, which apparently he had, that he would give the child something to make it sleep so it would never wake again. It seems the baby cried a lot at night and drove him to distraction. Then in an effort to cite extenuating circumstances he said that he had a fit in Bath Street 30 minutes before the incident and 'did not know what he was about'. In point of fact he was subject to epileptic fits, suffering one while he was attending the inquest at the *Two Anchors* in Guinea Street the following Tuesday afternoon.

Meanwhile, the mother and child were taken to the General Hospital where the child died within 2½ hours. John Mason, the attendant surgeon, said he had 'found the head much injured and swollen'. He discovered the skull to be fractured with part of the brain protruding. He had no doubt that death was caused by these injuries.

Because of Cann's fit – a severe one – it took three or four men to hold him down, so the inquest was adjourned until the Wednesday.

The first witness to be called on that day was Elizabeth Bird who was a widow who lodged in the same house as the Cann family. The house was owned by a Mr Strickland who lived there with his son, Thomas. She recalled a day about a fortnight back when the child was screaming and Mrs Cann had confided that her husband had blown tobacco smoke into its face. The Saturday before, at around 8 o'clock in the morning, she had heard the child crying and Mrs Cann say 'Don't, John. Don't beat the child. Don't hurt the child'. She went into the room to help and saw Mrs Cann sitting in a chair holding the baby. As she cried 'Don't hurt the child!' John Cann threw a boot at his wife which hit her on the nose. Mrs Cann then ran to Mrs Bird and handed the baby to her. It was covered with blood flowing from its mother's nose. Mrs Bird took the baby downstairs and Mrs Cann went back into her room where she could soon be heard to call out 'Murder!'.

Another lodger in the house, Esther Bennett, whose husband Asher was a labourer, had not seen Cann 'ill-use the child' but she had seen bruises on it which Mrs Cann had said that her husband had caused. Mrs Bennett stated that she had often heard Mrs Cann beg her husband not to beat the child and had, herself, frequently to call in neighbours to take the child from the prisoner when it was left alone with him. He had been heard to slap it on many occasions and it 'would cry very much afterwards'. She thought, from the prisoner's general manner towards the child that he had a dislike to it; had thought so ever since the child was born. She added that he was in the habit of staying out late and that he would go out in the morning leaving his wife without money or food.

It took but a few moments for the jury to return a verdict of 'Wilful Murder'.

As has been stated the trial took place the following April in Gloucester. Mr Skinner and Mr Dowdeswell conducted the prosecution and Mr Huddlestone defended the prisoner.

Thomas Williams was first to give his evidence, followed by the arresting officer, John Lee, who described events leading up to the arrest. He said he had known the child since soon after its birth but did not know its name. Another officer, Robert Keating, said that he had seen the accused several times during the evening in question. Was he, perhaps, the officer to whom John Lee had entrusted the care of Elizabeth Cann and her dying daughter? The custody officer, William Harris, then testified how Cann had drawn him into a discussion as to how much of the action Lee had actually witnessed.

Thomas Strickland, the landlord's son, was then called and he described a day in November when he returned home to find Cann beating the child. He had intervened. Elizabeth Cann was not at home at the time. When she returned she comforted the baby girl but it was heard crying again later. The next door neighbours also testified to witnessing John Cann maltreating his daughter.

Catherine Pearce was the next to take the stand. She told the court that she lived at 38 Redcliffe Street and that her husband, a butcher, worked for John Cann. She said his wife often brought the child to their home. At this point Cann was seized with another of his fits but fortunately there were enough medical men attending the trial to offer immediate assistance and Cann soon recovered and the trial continued.

Mrs Pearce admitted that she had seen bruises on the baby 'like the marks of knuckles' but, she said, 'I have never heard him say anything particular about the child'. Her husband, John, followed her into the witness box and repeated, almost word for word, what Catherine had said. It was at this juncture he was cautioned and reminded that he had been examined before. He then admitted he had heard the prisoner say he did not like his wife and child and he had also confided that his father had said if he would leave his wife he would advance him money to set him up in business.

Mr Mason, the surgeon who had given evidence regarding the child's injuries, was recalled and questioned about epilepsy. He said that a person, after having a fit like the prisoner might do things without knowing what he was doing, sometimes recovery taking longer than at other times.

Mr Huddlestone then addressed the jury and pointed out the various options – wilful murder, manslaughter, acquittal on the grounds of insanity, or complete acquittal. This was followed up by a summing up from the judge who read over the entire evidence. The jury consulted for a short time and then said they had reached a verdict of manslaughter.

In passing sentence His Lordship said:

> *You have been found guilty of manslaughter by the jury after a careful investigation. I think the jury have come to a proper conclusion for, to my mind, there is no evidence of your insanity. It would be dangerous to have it go out to this world that persons should commit these offences and that, because they are subject to epileptic fits, that they are to escape punishment. If they had found you guilty of murder, nobody, I believe, would have interfered to save your life. A more diabolical crime than yours I have scarcely ever had before me. It is quite clear that you had a most deliberate intention to destroy this child and I think you are the sort of man that, if you were out today, your wife would not be safe.*

The sentence of transportation for life was then passed on John Cann.

His Lordship then called up the two witnesses, Catherine and John Pearce and, having read over to them the depositions they swore before the magistrates, gave them a severe lecture on their prevarications and told them that he had a very good mind to commit them both for a month.

As in the case of Louisa Ferris, no trace has actually been made of John Cann being transported but it is to be hoped he never returned to Bristol to inflict further suffering on his poor wife.

CHAPTER 4

The Licentious Landlord
1851

All the accepted remedies were in vain . . .

As 1851 drew to a close in Kingswood, Gloucestershire, a village not far from Wootton-under-Edge, the area was rife with rumours relating to a resident of the locality who had died the previous October.

The person in question was Eliza Hart who, together with her husband, Henry, ran a beerhouse called *The King's Arms*. Henry, a baker by trade, incorporated this business with running the pub. Eliza and Henry had been married for many years although not very happily, especially latterly. The main cause of dissension was a young woman called Sarah Daniel who frequently used to call at the house and appeared equally friendly towards both husband and wife. Eliza, however, held deep suspicions about Sarah's motivation and was convinced there was more to the relationship between her husband and the young neighbour than he would acknowledge.

Towards the end of October Mrs Hart succumbed to a severe cold which she attributed to going out into the cold air after working in the hot steamy atmosphere of the bakehouse, for she was also involved in that side of Henry's business as well as her bar duties. All the accepted remedies were tried in vain; not only did they fail to alleviate the cold symptoms but she was also now plagued with violent stomach pains and vomiting.

Eliza Hart was forced to take to her bed. She had a sister, a Mrs Hooper, who lived in the neighbourhood who devoted much of her time to nursing her sister and, of course, Sarah Daniel was never far from the scene, calling on a daily basis with food to tempt the invalid. She brought some gruel she had prepared and persuaded Eliza to try some. After initial resistance Eliza said: 'Well, if I am to have it, let me have it at once.'

It is unclear whether or not she benefited from the gruel. Later one witness said it made her very ill, others swore to the contrary.

On another occasion Sarah made the trip into Gloucester specifically to purchase some biscuits for Eliza which she made up into food which she thought the patient would be able to eat. Again reports varied as to the effects these biscuits had on Eliza's digestive system. Some said she was ill after eating them, others refuted the suggestion.

Whatever the case, one thing is certain, Eliza became steadily worse and worse and Mr Hill, the Wootton surgeon was called in and attended her for 2 days. By this time her symptoms were constant thirst and a total inability to take any kind of solid food. When he could see she was making no improvement under his care, Mr Hill decided to seek a second opinion and sent for Mr Roberts of Wickwar in the hope that he could find a remedy which would bring about a change in her condition. Sadly, Mr Roberts also failed to find the cause of her problem or a cure and she died shortly afterwards.

Perhaps if Henry Hart and Sarah Daniel had acted a little more circumspectly at this stage nothing further would have been said but, 6 weeks after the burial of his wife, Henry Hart married Sarah, 'to the surprise and indignation of the neighbours'. In view of the haste with which the union took place, it is hardly surprising that Eliza Hart's relations, described as being 'of a very respectable family' were up in arms and the suspicion that had been lurking beneath the surface that Eliza's death may have been hastened in some way became an open topic for discussion. Eliza's relatives stated quite blatantly that they believed foul play by Miss Daniel had taken place. The whole business was dissected at length and it was remembered that when the body was placed in the coffin it appeared very swollen and discoloured. Mr Hill's opinion was sought but he said he had seen nothing in the complaint of the deceased to lead him to believe that anything of that nature was amiss.

Undeterred the family continued their crusade and a formal application was made to Mr W Joyner-Ellis, the coroner, 'for the purpose of examining the body and submitting it to a medical examination', but Mr Joyner-Ellis refused to order an exhumation without substantial evidence.

Dissatisfaction was displayed towards this refusal by both Eliza's relations and her friends and one of Eliza's sisters who hailed from North Nibley and had visited Eliza the day before her death openly declared she believed Eliza had been poisoned. The 'principal inhabitants' of the district, the press informed us, took the case up and so much noise was made about the matter that the coroner bowed to public demand and an inquest was arranged.

The inquest took place in the *Dog and Badger* and was packed to capacity. A 'most respectable jury, composed of magistrates and principal persons of the district', was sworn in and the ensuing examination was 'a very long one'. A large number of witnesses were examined, principally relatives and neighbours of the deceased but the evidence given was contradictory in the extreme. None of them agreed in any material statement to the point that the coroner declared he was 'never more dissatisfied in his life with any evidence than that given'.

Not a single witness had seen poison purchased or administered and although one woman swore Eliza had been sick after partaking of Sarah's gruel and of two pills Miss Daniel had given her, her niece 'distinctly swore that no ill effects followed'.

Even the medical men could not concur in their judgment. Mr Hill expressed a strong conviction that further examination was necessary because he could not account for the death from the symptoms he had observed during the 2 days he had attended her; Mr Roberts felt there was no reason to suspect the woman had not died from natural causes. To complicate matters further the post mortem ordered by the coroner had not taken place and the stomach contents remained unanalysed.

After listening to all these confusing testimonies the jury sensibly decided that a higher opinion should be sought and that the stomach of the deceased should be secured and sent to Mr Herapath in Bristol for his expert analysis and this was duly done and the inquest adjourned.

Even this decisive move, though, produced no concrete proof. The chemist made his examination and was able to confirm there was no trace of mineral poisons but, he added, 'there was some uncertainty with respect to vegetable poison, as from the circumstance of all vegetable poisons passing off from the system very rapidly, it is rendered much more difficult to detect'.

So, even then, the mystery remained unsolved. No doubt in the years that followed everyone in the village rarely cast a glance in the direction of Henry Hart and his second wife without the thought flitting across their minds: 'Did she or didn't she?' Whatever the truth of the matter was any secrets Sarah had she took to the grave.

The Dog and Badger *where the inquest on Eliza Hart took place.* Lewis Wilshire collection

CHAPTER 5

A Hullabaloo at Hinton Blewett
1852

He felt that the body had been lying in the well at least a month.

In October 1852 the papers were full of details of the funeral of national hero the Duke of Wellington. A list of those who would have their seats reserved in St Paul's Cathedral was published and details of the ceremony revealed. The body was to be covered with a 'rich black velvet pall adorned with escutcheons' and the carriage would be drawn by twelve horses decorated with trophies and heraldic achievements.

Closer to home, in Hinton Blewett, a Somerset hamlet close to Clutton, Temple Cloud, was also in the news. It had become

Cottages around the church. The author

The fields of Hinton Blewett. The author

the epicentre of a mystery which shook the residents and those of the neighbouring villages.

On Saturday 30 October John Plummer and Henry Dowling, two local labourers, were walking John's dog over the field known as Stony Ground. The dog ran over to the old well and began pulling at sticks which someone had used to cover the opening. The two men had a look and, endeavouring to replace the sticks, thought they could see something in the water. On closer inspection they were convinced it was a child. At this point an acquaintance of theirs, a man called Griffin, passed by and they called him over to verify what they believed they had seen. Griffin and Dowling remained on the spot while Plummer went off to fetch some well crooks to pull the body from the water.

The mission was successful and the baby was placed in a basket and carried to the belfry of the church where it was

One of the inns in Thomas Street close to where Sophia worked at the Three Queens.
C F W Dening, *The Old Inns of Bristol*

examined by James Dedden Perrin, a surgeon from Temple Cloud. He judged the child, a girl, to be about 6 weeks old and seemed to have been in the water several weeks to judge by the decomposition. There were wounds on the head and the back which possibly had been caused after death as the body was flung into the well.

Naturally rumours ran rife. It was remembered that Sophia Paine, erstwhile resident of the village had given birth a few months back. It was also remembered that, a while ago, she had visited her brother Jesse, who was employed at Savage's farm, carrying a bundle. It was reported that she had told him the baby was dead and tied up in the bundle.

Sophia now lived in Bristol, in bustling Thomas Street which had more than its fair share of hostelries. She had been cook at the *Three Queens Tavern* but, since the birth of her daughter, had been working as a dressmaker.

Both Sophia and Jesse were obvious suspects and were arrested. In fact, after her arrest gossip had it that she had been heard to say she had come to see Jesse between 2 and 3 months ago. It was said she told him she had given the baby some laudanum because it was crying and fretful and she had accidentally given it too much and the baby had died. She then panicked and wanted him to help her bury it but he refused. It was then, in a state of terror, it was reported that she threw the body down the well. None of this information could be verified, however.

The inquest took place at the *Seven Stars*, Hinton, before magistrate R Ashford. Sophia had been apprehended in Bristol. Mr James Dedden Perrin (surgeon) gave a detailed description of the child's injuries and stomach contents. He spoke of the decomposition, which was not so far advanced as to prevent him detecting external marks of violence. On the left side of the forehead, about an inch above the ear, 'was a semi-circular incisive wound of the integuments . . .' (skin) 'about the size of a half-crown piece, and which extended through the whole of the scalp, so as to lay bare the bone; the edges of the wound were filled with dirt; there was a bloody exudation from the nose'. He admitted it was similar to the exudation that follows drowning and was not from decomposition. He had also found a mark between the nose and upper lip, the tongue partially protruded and there were bruises on the body, one on the back.

He described the lungs as being in a healthy state and they were filled with air and although the liver and stomach were entirely decomposed the intestines were not so badly damaged and he was able to ascertain there was no trace of laudanum therein. He was not able to say for certain how death occurred. He had opened the head and found the brain to be one mass of matter, which ran away in a fluid state. The faeces were healthy and there was no sign of constipation or lack of bile. He felt if the drug had been administered the tests he made would have detected it. He felt the body had been lying in the well at least a month.

The coroner returned to the subject of the laudanum because Sophia's supposed story seemed to hinge on this aspect. He asked Mr Dedden Perrin if there were any instances in which the drug had been discovered long after death. The surgeon replied that not in the case of laudanum but its product morphia and it was for this he had tested. In the majority of cases, he said, it might be detected irrespective of time and went on to explain that one French writer had stated that he could detect it even in a particle long after death. Again the body blows were discussed and it was confirmed that, after such a time had elapsed, it was impossible to judge whether or not they had occurred before or after death.

The coroner then queried if a mineral poison been administered, and whether or not the intestines would have been inflamed. The surgeon countered this by saying that the state of the facial matter ruled out the possibility of this type of poison being used.

Jesse Paine was then cautioned and gave his deposition, explained he was a labourer in the employ of farmer Savage 'of this village'. He said that his sister, Sophia, had come to see him at the farm about a month ago. She came first, he said, at about 10 o'clock at night but he was not at home. She returned a little later 'with a relative named Maria Paine'. His sister had requested he go to Hinton Down with her, although she did not explain why. She carried a bundle under her arm. He went with her and as they walked she revealed her story: 'She then told me she had had a child', said Jesse 'and asked me what she was to do with it; I told her I did not know, that she could do what she liked with it; I said "It is nothing to I, and I'll have no hands in it." I then left her and saw no more of her afterwards till this day; I did not go to the stony ground field; when she left me she had this bundle with her; when she talked about the child, she told me that she had it in her bundle; she said that it was dead but did not say how long before it had died.'

He told the inquest that Sophia had not told him how the child's death had come about, neither did he ask. She also gave no indication to him what she intended doing with it. Apparently Maria was not present when any of the discussion was taking place as she had gone off and left the two of them to their business.

The coroner then asked him if he had stated to someone 'in this parish' that he had seen his sister throw the child into the well. He gave the reply: 'No, folks run about with stories, but it is no good my saying what I did not see.'

The coroner then remarked that the witness appeared to have given his evidence in a very straightforward manner, and as a report of his having seen the child thrown down the well had gone abroad, he thought it was due to him that any persons who had stated it should come forward and state the grounds of the report. The foreman of the jury agreed the young man had given his evidence very fairly.

Maria Paine was then called. She said Sophia was a distant relative of hers and 'a month ago last Monday she had come to her house and had tea'. Afterwards Sophia asked her to walk up the hill with her and they walked up to farmer Savage's place. Sophia was carrying a bundle with her. They waited an hour for Jesse and when he finally arrived they all walked together to Hinton, speaking of nothing in particular. When they came to the green she left them and walked home alone. She confirmed that Sophia had never mentioned to her that she had had a child, nor did she say what was in the bundle. Later on Sophia returned to Maria's house and slept the night there. She no longer had the bundle in her possession. Maria noticed nothing remarkable about her dress or appearance. The next morning, after breakfast, Sophia took herself off for the day, returning in the evening and again sleeping at Maria's, as, indeed, she did the following night. Maria recalled that when she first arrived at the house Maria's mother asked her to put the bundle down but Sophia would not do so and kept it on her arm the whole time. She overheard her mother enquiring what was in the bundle to which Sophia replied 'game' and that she wanted to see Jesse.

The coroner interrupted at this juncture to announce that he had received information which led him to believe the young woman, the prisoner, 'had called at the *Pelican Inn*, Chew Magna, with her child and that same person had also purchased laudanum at the same village' and he had sent a constable there. However, Charles Stallard, landlord of the inn, when called, firmly stated that the prisoner was not that woman.

Apparently the drug had been purchased from a man called Milton but he did not recollect to whom he had sold it and therefore would not attend the proceedings. This caused a bit of annoyance on the part of the coroner who said the man could be held in contempt of court but then it was discovered that the constable had not served the summons so Milton was in the clear. The inquest was then adjourned.

The following Tuesday proceedings were resumed and the prisoner, who had been held in custody at the *Seven Stars Inn*, was brought in 'that she might have an opportunity of hearing what the witnesses said'. Sophia was described in the press as 'very respectably attired' and 'possessed considerable personal attractions'.

The first witness to be called was Hannah Houghton the wife of a Bristol haulier. Sophia had lodged with her for 8 weeks and had left 5 or 6 weeks ago. During the time she lived there she had given birth to a daughter who was healthy and 'very fine' in all that time. The child's usual mode of dress was a flannel night-gown and little shirt but no cap or bonnet. Sophia had spoken several times about registering the baby but Mrs Houghton didn't believe she had ever actually done so. Eventually she said she was taking the child to an aunt in the country to be nursed. She went away one Monday morning and Mrs Houghton had not seen her since. Some clothes were produced for the witness to examine, those in which the dead child had been found, but Mrs Houghton said she could not identify any of them.

Eliza Sams, was then called to give her deposition. She and her husband, John, kept the *Prince Albert* beerhouse, situated next door to the Houghtons' house and said she knew Sophia Paine. She recalled that 5 or 6 weeks ago Sophia had called at her house between 10 and 11 o'clock one Monday morning to borrow a shawl to wrap the baby in, saying she was taking it to her aunt's to be nursed. Mrs Sams was not positive whereabouts the aunt lived but did remember some mention being made of 'Easton, near Bath'. That Friday Sophia called again at Mrs Sams' house and did not have the baby with her then. On being asked how it was she replied 'quite well'. Mrs Sams remembered the child appearing to be in good health the last time she saw her although it had been poorly from time to time since its birth.

Elizabeth Webley then took the stand and said that she had known the prisoner for about 5 months and was present when the baby girl was born 'about 8 or 9 weeks yesterday'. She said that after 3 weeks Sarah took it away 'to be nursed'. She, too, was unable to identify the baby clothes in which the dead child had been found.

The druggist from Chew Magna was then called but could not identify Sophia Paine as someone to whom he had sold laudanum, qualifying this by adding there were a large number of persons who came to his shop to purchase this item. Laudanum was a popular means in those days to quieten a restless child.

The next witness was Elisha Horner who said he was a labourer and worked for a man called Wright. He had accompanied the constable who had travelled to Bristol the previous week to arrest Sophia. The coroner asked him if the prisoner had made any voluntary statement during the journey to which Horner replied: 'She said she had a child and she was coming out to put the child to nurse,' adding that the child had proved restless and she gave it a few drops of laudanum and afterwards could not awaken it although she threw water in its face. Horner said she had told him she was very much alarmed when she found the child would not wake up and 'did not know what to

The Ring o' Bells – *now Hinton Blewett's only pub.* Author's collection

do about having it buried'. He told the inquest that she said she went to her brother in the evening to try and have it buried at which point Sophia assailed him with the words: 'Don't you tell no more lies, Horner, to please no one.'

The next witness was Henry Barwell, a coal miner from Bishop Sutton. He said he knew Sophia and saw her about 5 or 6 weeks ago at a beer house in the village. She had asked him to walk up the hill with her as it was dark and he walked 'three parts of the way to Hinton with her'. She tried to persuade him to go with her the whole journey, saying she would treat him to a quart of beer but he refused. He noticed she was carrying a bundle and offered to carry it for her but she refused. She said she was going to carry it up to her child at Hinton. He left her then and had not seen her since.

Thomas Lovell, the constable who had been sent to Bristol to bring Sophia in, said he had met her in the street and she had 'made no resistance' but came 'very willingly'. On the way back she told him she had had a child and her intention was to take it out to her aunt to keep in the country but it had become very restless and troublesome on the journey and she gave it a little laudanum to keep it quiet but not with any intention to injure it. She seemed, said PC Lovell, 'rather low spirited'.

The coroner then cleared the room and summed up the evidence after which the jury convened for 30 minutes to deliver the verdict 'Found dead, but how the deceased came by its death there is no evidence to show'.

The coroner then ordered the prisoner to be released and the proceedings terminated.

And so Sophia Paine, possessor of 'considerable personal attractions' faded back into obscurity leaving us to wonder how the rest of her life was spent after this traumatic event.

CHAPTER 6

A Dastardly Deed at Dundry
1861

She had been beaten savagely about the head ...

The weekly newspaper of the day, the *Bristol Times* and Felix Farley's *Bristol Journal* of Saturday 12 January 1861 used the headline 'Murder, Outrage and Robbery at Dundry'. The event being described was 'a most brutal murder, atrocious assault and heartless robbery' which had been 'perpetrated at Dundry, a village about 6 miles from this city'. The attack was carried out on the previous Wednesday and the victims were George and Sarah Waterman, aged 75 and 73 respectively. They are described as being quiet, inoffensive people who owned the cottage in which they lived plus about an acre of land which they farmed and kept a cow, enabling Mr Waterman to establish a milk round. Their cottage lay in a hollow, the roof being only slightly above road level. It was a comparatively new building commanding a fine view from its position on the side of Winford Hill. Apparently it was relatively isolated, there being only one other building nearby and that half-finished. The cottage was reached by a flight of rugged winding steps then a stile had to be scaled and finally a visitor would reach a pathway which led to the front of the house. Generally, however, a doorway which led into the scullery was used and from there, through another door, the kitchen was accessed.

At about 7 o'clock that night the couple were sitting by the kitchen fire, Mrs Waterman busy with her sewing, when there came a knock upon the door. George called out to ask who was there and received the reply 'It's John, the Winford policeman'. However, when he opened the door two men were there and the

The slopes of Winford Hill where the Watermans' cottage stood. The author

shorter of the two attacked George with a stout stick. He was then hustled upstairs and asked to produce money and valuables, then forced back down the stairs and into the adjoining milkhouse where they bound him, tying him to the leg of a bacon stand. They instructed him to remain where he was for 20 minutes, then he could call his wife to let him loose. They returned to the main part of the house. Although very weak from loss of blood, George managed to free himself and made his way to the kitchen where he found Sarah unconscious on the floor. He tried to lift her but it was was too much for him so he went out of the cottage and made his way to his nearest neighbour, William Lovell, a butcher who lived about 200–300 yards away. Lovell helped him back and was shocked at the sight of Mrs Waterman stretched out on the kitchen floor, bleeding profusely from several wounds. He rushed off to fetch further assistance and the poor woman was carried up to bed while a messenger was despatched to alert Mr Shorland, a surgeon who lived locally. He rushed to the cottage and treated the dreadful head wounds but she was beyond human help and died about 9.30 without having gained consciousness. At this stage it was not known when she actually suffered the attack as her husband did not hear her call out but it was thought she had tried to come to his aid and had been beaten off in her attempts. It looked as if the instrument used was the fire tongs as they bore traces of blood and a small quantity of human hair.

The police were then informed, suspicion already falling on Mrs Waterman's two nephews, Charles and Matthew Wedmore. By the following evening they had been apprehended in Hotwells 'through the activity and vigilance of two Bristol detectives, police constables Perrott and Hughes'. The Wedmores resisted arrest, attempting to shoot the officers. It seemed they had gone straight into Bristol after committing the murder and had done the rounds of local public houses. They had tried to sell some of the goods stolen from the Watermans'

The Rummer *in High Street Market. William Lovell, a butcher and neighbour of the Watermans remembered seeing Charles Wedmore 2 or 3 months prior to the murder in a tavern in the market.* C F W Dening, *The Old Inns of Bristol*

home which included 'two old-fashioned silver watches, with cases, one with a piece of twine attached, and a bull's-eye glass cracked across the middle; the other with a black riband attached; a brace of pistols, a little worn and of percussion make; a bottle of brandy, some bottles of home-made wine, 5 or 6 shillings in silver, some bacon, cheese and a loaf of bread'.

They had actually persuaded a woman to pledge one of the watches for them. After their arrest they were taken to Clifton police station. Apparently they were strong, muscular men and had recently been living with a married sister, a Mrs Hill, who lived in Jones Court, Hotwell Road, a cluster of tightly packed dwellings not far from the *Spring Gardens Tavern*. After the Wedmores were locked up a further arrest was made – that of Harriet Francis who lived in a court in Jacob's Wells who was charged with having in her possession part of the property stolen from the house on the night of the murder. They searched her house and found some bread, cheese and bacon which she said she had bought at the door but she was not believed. The prisoners were also subjected to a search at the police station and found to be in possession of a canvas bag purse similar to one thought to have been taken together with the rest of the haul from the Dundry cottage.

George Waterman was pronounced by John Shorland to be in 'a very dangerous state from blows on the head producing extensive lacerated wounds and he may not be able to give evidence at any future time. He is perfectly sensible now'.

George Waterman then gave his deposition knowing that 'I may not recover'. He described hearing the knock on the door at 7 o'clock on the evening of 9 January and on enquiring who was there received the reply 'John, the Winford policeman'. He related how he was attacked and forced upstairs, by which time he had been struck several times on the head. Among the items they took was 'a Waterloo medal with riband and three silver bars attached'. He then recounted how he was dragged downstairs, forced to pack up some food for them and then the shorter of the two men bound his hands and forced him into the milkhouse and fastened him to the bacon stand.

He remembered that while being struck he had begged the men to spare his wife and was told 'I have put her to sleep.'

He then described how he managed to free himself and go for help. He was able to describe his assailants and thought he would recognise them again, especially the shorter man whom he believed he had seen before that night: he 'wore hair under his chin. He was a young man, about 35 years of age. I noticed that the taller man had a thin pale face. He wore a large jacket like a shooting jacket, with large inside pockets'. Having taken possession of the pistols the taller man threatened Mr Waterman.

The next stage of the procedure sounds rather barbaric but this was the norm at the time of this case. The two prisoners were conveyed to the police station at Bourton and placed in the custody of the county police who took them to Dundry to confront the injured man. A crowd gathered outside the house while this part of the proceedings took place. Waterman then made a sworn statement that these were the men who committed the outrage.

Meanwhile the inquest on Sarah Waterman was opened at the *Dundry Inn* which, it is reported was 'crowded to excess'. The coroner was Bruges Fry Esq. and the foreman of the jury of fourteen was the Reverend C W M Boutflower. The coroner explained that he was not in possession of the full facts at this stage and, like the jury, had only heard various reports and rumours regarding the men in custody so they were to banish from their minds all that they had heard and confine themselves

View from the rear of the Dundry Inn *showing the original structure. The initial hearing into the death of Sarah Waterman was held here.* The author

entirely to the evidence before them. The jury then viewed the body and afterwards were told that, as the chief witness, George Waterman had made a sworn declaration as to the identity of the men in custody, the prisoners would be brought before the jury and confronted with the witnesses. The statement was read out at the inquest.

First to be called was William Lovell who said that he knew the deceased, Sarah Waterman, whom, he thought to be aged 73 or thereabouts and had last seen her, in perfect health, when he 'sat half an hour in their company' at 3 o'clock on the Thursday prior to the murder. He told how Waterman came to his house on the evening of the 9th saying 'My wife is murdered and I am almost'. Lovell, not understanding quite what he was hearing asked him what exactly had happened and Waterman said 'Two ruffians have been and murdered my missus and almost me'. Lovell went on to describe walking George Waterman back to his cottage and discovering Sarah lying on the floor 'covered with blood'. He managed to lift her into an armchair before going to 'Batt's public house', by which he meant the *Dundry Inn*, to raise the alarm and to send for Mr Shorland, the surgeon.

William Lovell had already encountered the two men earlier on the evening in question in the tap room at the *Dundry Inn* and had sat near them although did not engage in conversation with them. He had recognised 'the taller man', Charles Wedmore, having seen him before 2 or 3 months previously at the *Crown Tap*, High Street Market in Bristol.

John Shorland then took the stand, giving his address as Dundry Grove, Somerset. He described at length Sarah Waterman's horrendous injuries. She had been beaten savagely about the head and when the surgeon arrived he found she had 'heavy sonorous breathing and the pupil of the left eye was fully dilated and perfectly insensible to the strongest light that could be thrown upon it'. He attempted to administer brandy but she was unable to swallow and her pulse was very feeble. Her dress was saturated in blood and her head wounds were severe and had clearly been struck with great force and with a blunt instrument. He had her taken upstairs to her bed but she died within the hour, said Shorland, 'in all probability from compression

Looking up the slopes to the Dundry Inn *in times past.* Dundry.org.uk

of the brain caused by extravasation of blood, produced by violence; I think all the injuries must have been inflicted by very heavy blows'.

After George Waterman's testimony was read the coroner and jury had to go to the cottage for him to sign it in the presence of the jury. Some additional evidence had come to light and he made a statement to the effect that a silver watch recovered by Henry Calcott of the Bristol police force was his property. Recovering a little now from the initial shock, he had recalled that Charles Wedmore had called at the house on Friday 4 January, 5 days before the murder.

Back in the *Dundry Inn* the hearing continued with PC Calcott describing how the watch had been handed to him by Jeremiah Jordan, landlord of the *Thetis Frigate* beerhouse in Tower Lane, Bristol.

Jeremiah Jordan then told his part of the story. He said the two prisoners had come to his place the day before between 9 and 10 o'clock. He did not recall ever having seen either of them before. They ordered a quart of beer and asked if 'Cocker' was at home, 'Cocker' being a man who lodged at the beer-house. Cocker came down with 'his woman' and they were joined by Jordan's maidservant, Mary Ann Cullen. Matthew Wedmore then produced a watch and asked Jordan 'Will you pawn a watch for me, as we can trust you before we can any of the girls?'. Jordan took the watch and Mary Ann pawned it but Jordan redeemed it and handed it to the police. Another watch was also produced on that morning by Matthew but that had not yet turned up.

The pistols and the house keys were then produced by Police Sergeant Morse of the Somerset constabulary and PC Perrott of Bristol as being found in the possession of the prisoners and the jury were told they had been identified by George Waterman. The arrest was then described including the disarming of the two young men.

The newspaper report states that the prisoners remained perfectly silent during the enquiry 'seeming to regard the proceedings with some degree of curiousity'. Charles Wedmore is described as being 'a fine, active and intelligent looking young man' although Matthew 'has a rather sullen and repulsive appearance'. They were dressed in the garb of common labourers and 'looked as though they had lately been working in a colliery'.

The trial took place at Taunton in March and Matthew who was aged 34 and Charles, aged 28, both pleaded not guilty.

George Waterman had made a remarkable recovery and was living with his nephew, Thomas Waterman in North Ward Street, Glastonbury. With his renewed strength he was able to give a more detailed account of the events of the night of 9 January. He recalled now that when he was frogmarched up to the bedroom and the pistols were discovered Charles had aimed the weapon at him saying to his brother 'Take him and kill him; we don't mind killing people'. The fact then emerged that the men were his great nephews, their mother being his sister's daughter.

With the evidence piling up against them as the witnesses gave their damning depositions a statement was produced given by Charles Wedmore whilst in custody at Long Ashton police station on 14 January 1861. In it he described how the two of them had gained access to the Watermans' house on the night of 9 January. He admitted Matthew had struck a blow as soon as the door was opened and that George Waterman then ran inside and picked up the tongs and turned to face Matthew whereupon he suffered the full force of Matthew's violence. Charles then stood over the injured man who had fallen to his knees as his brother went in pursuit of Sarah who was trying to reach the back door. He struck her several times on the head saying 'You —————, I will kill you'. Charles said he had said to his brother 'Do not kill her' and Matthew proceeded to drag her into the kitchen and leave her on her side on the floor. He then grabbed George's collar and instructed the man to 'show us where the money is', hustling the man up the stairs. He described the actual robbery and what spoils they carried away and said they had left the old man tied to the bacon stand. Apparently, while in Taunton Gaol Matthew had made a voluntary statement to the same effect except he placed the blame and the entire escapade firmly at his brother's door, saying that it was his idea.

Their defence counsel contended that the charge of murder had not been legally established and that the statements 'alleged to have been made by the prisoners' had been withheld from the defence but his words fell on deaf ears and the jury after 'a brief deliberation' returned a verdict of guilty. It is said that the two prisoners betrayed no emotion throughout the trial.

The execution of the Wedmore brothers was scheduled for 5 April 1861. In the days leading up to their death there was 'a change for the better in the demeanour of the two men and both appeared to become at length aware of the awful position in which they stood'. Matthew is described as having a strange, vacant smile on his face during this time and it was generally agreed that he was the main perpetrator of the crime. Charles was thought to be a less daring and more impressionable character, easily manipulated by someone with a stronger and more vicious nature. It was Charles, too, who was the main object of concern to their mother who lived at Failand and was heard to declare that she would crawl on her hands and knees to the place of execution and take his place if it were possible to save him from being hanged. She and her late husband had always been considered decent and peaceable people who earned their living by the sale, in Clifton, of rabbits obtained from the warrens of the Smythes. Two of their daughters, both respectable young women, were in service in the Clifton area.

A few of the Wedmores' friends visited to say farewell and then, on the day when they were to pay the ultimate penalty for their crime they were escorted to the chapel to take communion then conducted to the scaffold. Outside the Shire Hall and County Gaol a large crowd had gathered which included a large percentage of women and children. Matthew died without a struggle but Charles gave a few convulsive throes. They were buried within the precincts of the gaol, a short distance from the spot where the infamous John Beale, murderer of Charlotte Pugsley, had been interred 3 years previously.

CHAPTER 7

Illegitimacy and Infanticide
1863

... it was a battle of wills between the jury and the coroner.

The Victorian era was probably one in which more unwanted babies met untimely ends than in any other period in history. Victoria's long reign was one in which strong moral values had to be seen to prevail and temperance movements and philanthropic ventures were the order of the day.

Beneath the surface, though, reality was very different. Child pornography was rife and women sold their bodies for a few pence to avoid starvation. The poor lived in appalling conditions, in overcrowded and verminous courts and hovels praying they could earn enough to keep themselves and their families out of the workhouse. If a girl became pregnant outside marriage the shame of the situation would often drive her to extreme measures.

The three girls who found themselves in this position in 1863 were Annie Mortimer, Elizabeth Ann Targett and Mary Ann Golding. A fourth, Martha Fifoot, lost her child in a moment of drunken carelessness. They were tried at two different courts and received very different treatment. It is hard to believe this attitude was not dependent upon their social status.

Annie was the daughter of Richard Mortimer, manager of the Keynsham Brass Mills. It is intriguing to speculate on the affair that precipitated her actions on to that day in May when she locked herself in her room for 7 hours. When she was eventually persuaded to open the door a dead baby was found on her bed, lying on the mattress under the bedclothes.

From the very outset the entire investigation seems to have been handled with kid gloves. Miss Mortimer failed to put in an

The house where Annie Mortimer lived adjacent to the brass mills. Photograph courtesy of Amanda Britton

The Keynsham brass mills where Annie's father was manager. Photograph courtesy of Amanda Britton

appearance at the coroner's inquest although the jury were insistent she attended. The coroner waived the instruction so that no accusation could be levelled against her. Afterwards the police were forced to take charge and she was taken into custody.

The post-mortem was carried out by Keynsham surgeon Robert Nash assisted by a Bristol doctor, James Foxwell. Their findings were that Anne had given birth to a healthy and fully mature male child. There were no outward signs of violence. The lungs were not fully expanded and when they were removed, together with the heart, and placed in water they floated. There was no disease and all the blood vessels were healthy as were all the internal organs. When the brain was removed a quantity of blood was discovered. The skull was not fractured but Nash thought the child had received an accidental blow to the head. He believed the baby to have been alive at birth but could not establish if it had actually drawn breath.

From then on it was a battle of wills between the jury and the coroner. At the adjourned hearing once again Annie's appearance was passed off by the coroner as 'not so important' and he stated his opinion that the evidence suggested only 'concealment of birth' which could not be entertained in a coroner's court. He suggested a verdict of 'Found dead' leaving the magistrates to proceed further in the matter and reiterated that the evidence would not support a charge of manslaughter.

The jury were not satisfied and insisted that they needed to talk the matter over for themselves whereupon the court was cleared and they were left to undertake a lengthy debate. Eventually they announced their verdict that 'the child's death was occasioned by wilful neglect'.

The coroner was aghast. He addressed the jury, saying 'Do you know, gentlemen, that that amounts to murder? That is not the verdict you intended I presume?' to which the foreman doggedly replied: 'The child died from wilful neglect. That is how every man brings it in.'

The coroner strove to gain ascendancy and said 'You are quite aware, I suppose, that this is at variance with the medical evidence?'

The foreman was not to be moved. He said firmly: 'The medical evidence is that the child was born alive; and the medical gentleman believes it would still have been alive if it had been properly cared for and attended. Therefore we consider it died from neglect.'

Mr Foxwell then explained at length the difference between respiring and being born alive, striving to influence the relentless panel of men before him and the coroner again pointed out the difference between murder and manslaughter and said the medical evidence was opposed to either. He asked them to reconsider their verdict. Murder or manslaughter?

The foreman answered 'Manslaughter'.

All attempts by the coroner to persuade the jury to back down had failed. He said: 'Then you intend to find a verdict of manslaughter? You believe that if the child had had proper care at birth it would have lived.'

'Yes,' replied the foreman, 'that is our opinion. We mean a verdict of manslaughter. We find that Annie Mortimer did feloniously kill and slay her infant male illegitimate child on 15 May.'

The coroner, who by this stage must have been almost choking with indignation, said he would make out her commitment to Taunton Gaol and he could not bring her before his court. He declared that he had no idea how such a verdict could be recorded in the teeth of the medical evidence.

At last Miss Mortimer was brought into the room and was cautioned. She declined to say anything. The coroner offered to take bail but it was not forthcoming.

Annie's trial took place on the same day as Elizabeth Ann Targett who had, for some time, been languishing in Wilton Gaol. She was a domestic servant who had been in the employ of a surgeon, a Mr Ford of Wedmore. His sister kept house for him. Elizabeth had started work there on 25 March 1863 but when it was discovered she was pregnant she was asked to leave. Before her departure could be arranged though a child was born to her. The baby was found in an outside lavatory in the yard by local policeman, Sergeant Noble. The inquest findings showed death was due to 'neglect' but the actual details relating to the condition of the body were deemed unfit for publication.

The inquest jury brought in a verdict of 'manslaughter' and Elizabeth was detained under a coroner's warrant in Wilton Gaol until Mr Hancock, the surgeon, decided she was fit to stand trial.

When Annie Mortimer made her appearance at Taunton Assizes the papers reported that she was 'fashionably dressed' and made her plea of 'Not Guilty' in a firm voice. The contrast was drawn with others in the dock that day, Elizabeth Ann Targett among them, that the 'others were not so respectably dressed'.

Regardless of the social chasm between Annie Mortimer and Elizabeth Ann Targett the outcome was the same. The jury could not find any true bill against either of them. The coroner's jury had found both guilty 'in point of reason' but their guilt was not so clear in a point of law. No further evidence was offered and so the prisoners were discharged.

It is interesting to ponder how Annie's life in Keynsham panned out in the aftermath of the scandal. Perhaps she was sent away to spend time with a relative until the gossip died down. Her chances of a successful marriage may well have been blighted.

And Elizabeth Ann? Without the details of her crime being made known it is hard to form an opinion of the extent of her actions but the fragility of her state of mind can never have been in question. The very fact of her being restrained under a warrant at Wilton Gaol until doctors declared her fit to stand trial gives a clear indication that she was in a disturbed state. What might have become of her when she was released into society once more?

Another servant girl who found herself in a similar situation in the summer of 1863 was Mary Ann Golding. Twenty-one-year-old Mary Ann who had been employed by a family in Chippenham, started work as a housemaid on 2 July for a Mr Anderson who owned Stapleton Road Villa, one of the new houses which had been built in the Eastville section of Stapleton Road, not far from the *Black Swan*. Mr Anderson's widowed sister, Mrs Prince, kept house for him and he also employed a cook by the name of Louisa Morgan.

The Black Swan *at Eastville. In a nearby house Mary Ann Golding was accused of killing her new-born baby.* Mike Tozer collection

On Thursday 16 July Mary Ann attended to her allotted tasks and waited on table as usual at 6 o'clock in the evening but failed to answer cook's summons at 7 o'clock to clear the table. Louisa Morgan went to investigate and found the girl in her room and she appeared 'rather excited'. When asked why she had not answered the summons she made no reply, merely leaving the room and making her way downstairs. Louisa noticed some marks on the floor which led her to look under the bed. There, crammed into a chamber pot, was a new-born baby, 'gasping for life and moving its legs; lying face uppermost'. She confronted Mary on the stairs asking what she had done but all the girl would say was 'Don't tell the missus.' Louisa said 'I must'.

Afterwards she and Mrs Prince went up to the room and Louisa tried to revive the baby but by this time there was no movement and she realised it was dead.

Mrs Prince was in some confusion as to the right course of action and ran next door to consult with her neighbours, the

Kings. She berated Mary Ann saying 'You are a very wicked girl; you should have told me the state you were in'. She then ordered her to pack up and leave immediately. Mr King intervened, saying it was a police matter and Mary Ann should remain until they had spoken to her.

The eminent pathologist, Mr William Herapath, was called to examine the child's body. When he arrived Mary Ann was sitting in her room, trunk packed and ready for departure. Of the baby there was no sign. She was asked for the key to her box and handed it over. There, inside, was the little body, wrapped in an apron and neatly packed away among the clothes.

When Mr Herapath proceeded with his examination he found scratches on the body made with either blunt scissors or fingernails, the skull was fractured which he believed to be the result of violence. He thought that this was the cause of death, hastened by the bleeding.

It is not recorded what Mary Ann said in her defence. She had made no preparations whatsoever for the birth; not a single item of babywear was found among her possessions. It was as if, by ignoring the situation, she hoped it might all go away.

The trial took place at Gloucester Assizes on 14 August. Mary Ann, described in contemporary reports as being 'showily dressed', was defended by a Mr Wightman who was insistent that the injuries could well have been accidental and that the prisoner was entitled to an acquittal on the charge of murder. He condemned the attitude of Mrs Prince in ordering her out of the house quoting sentimentally:

> For every sin forgiveness has a name
> Except an erring sister's shame.

The judge, summing up, expressed the opinion that the placing of the child in the box amounted to a concealment of birth; then, the question was, was this child born alive? If so, were the injuries wilful or the result of negligence and neglect? If it was the first then the charge was murder.

The jury consulted for some time, finally reaching a verdict of manslaughter as a result of the prisoner's negligence. Mary Ann was sentenced to 12 months' imprisonment with hard labour.

Later that day Martha Fifoot was brought into court to be indicted for the manslaughter of her infant child. A glance through police records of that era is enough to show that the Fifoot family, or at least one branch of it, were the sort of people who would be handed out ASBOs were they living in the twenty-first century.

Martha herself is described in the *Bristol Mercury* as being 'a woman of dissipated appearance'. She and her husband would certainly be deemed less than responsible parents. On the night in question, 27 April, the pair were in a two-wheeled trap together with about four friends. William Dowsing, a furniture broker who lived in Broadmead saw the trap pass his house at 7.30 and again at 8.45. He noticed Martha on the outside of the trap holding a baby and as they passed his house the second time saw the baby had fallen out. The second occasion the trap had passed, he said that it was travelling at speed and swaying from side to side, all the passengers appearing to be under the influence of drink.

Another witness, William Eddy, a bootmaker of Cherry Lane, said he had gone to meet the trap and saw the baby fall out whereupon he ran over and picked it up. Fifoot was driving at the time and driving very fast. He did not notice at the time whether or not Martha was drunk.

Dowsing was recalled and added that some lads were chasing after the trap and the vehicle was travelling so fast he was unable to see in what way the prisoner was holding the baby.

William Phelps was then called, having been brought up from Bristol Gaol to give evidence. He was one of those travelling in the trap but he had not noticed whether or not Martha was holding the baby. He did admit that Martha 'was not able to take care of herself'. He did hear some people yelling as they went past that someone had dropped a parcel and he alighted to pick it up before realising it was, in fact, Martha's baby. He, himself, was sober at the time. He took the baby to the infirmary but it was dead by the time he arrived there. He had no idea of the age of the child, only that it was 'in long clothes'.

At this stage the judge interposed. He said all the material parts of the evidence had been laid before the jury and he did not think it sufficient to support the charge of manslaughter.

The jury 'expressed themselves satisfied and acquitted the prisoner' who was immediately discharged.

Clearly the court did not consider this sort of parental neglect leading to the death of a child worthy of any sort of debate. It was almost as though people of these habits and life style were treated totally dismissively. In sharp contrast to Annie Mortimer's case where the coroner was anxious to sweep everything under the carpet to protect the good name of her wealthy family, the Fifoots and their friends were of so little importance that it mattered little to anyone whether they did accidentally kill their children when they had had a drop too much to drink.

CHAPTER 8

A Killing on the Quay
1875

She was covered in blood and barely conscious.

It was reported first as a 'serious assault' and it was on the charge of a 'violent assault' that Philip Morris, a powerfully-built man, over 6 feet tall, found himself up before the magistrates in April 1875. The men on the bench were H J Mills and William Hathway, a one-time mayor of the city.

Police Constable Capper, giving evidence, said he was informed at 2.15pm on the Monday in question that a woman named Morris had been badly beaten at her home, 82 Narrow Quay. Her assailant was her husband. When the officer arrived at the house he found the victim in bed, lying on her face and hands. She was covered in blood and barely conscious. He arranged for her to be conveyed to the infirmary where it was ascertained she had several wounds to the head and her skull was fractured. At that juncture little hope of recovery was being entertained.

Another lodger in the house, sailor's wife Sarah Beckett recalled that on the fateful Monday, about midday, a little girl called Mary Ann came knocking at the Morris' door. At length Morris came to the door and the following conversation was overheard.

Morris: 'Who's there?'

Mary Ann: 'Me.'

'Who's me?' asked Morris and the girl gave her name.

On being asked what she wanted she said her mother had sent her to collect the rent. Morris asked then how much was owed and the girl said '4 months', to which Morris's response

The quayside as it would have looked in Morris's day. Arrowsmith's Directory of Bristol, 1898

was 'Tell your mother that we have no rent; me and my wife are both drunk and we will try and get some rent in a day or two'.

The girl left and Sarah overheard Morris repeat three times '4 months, eh?' but she heard no screams. She reported that he then came out of the house and 'appeared to be very excited' – by which she clearly meant 'disturbed'.

At this juncture Mrs Morris's 9-year-old son came home and asked his mother how she 'came to be knocked about so'. First of all she said she 'did it herself' then afterwards admitted 'Morris did it'. The lad then went to Sarah's room and told her what had happened. Sarah Beckett expressed the view that the couple were both 'the worse for liquor' and said that when Mrs Morris had taken a drop too much she always went to bed to sleep it off.

Morris was arrested at his sister's house in Park Lane, off St Michael's Hill. The assault, it seemed, had been committed using a tailor's sleeve board.

When charged with the offence at the police station, Morris remarked to Inspector Riordan 'I have come here twice to complain of my wife; she's a thorough bad woman; I have been 25 years in the British Army and it's hard that I should be tied up with such a wretch'. Three times Morris enquired if his wife was dead and when the officer told him she was not he said 'If she's not dead, I'll dead her'.

At this stage reports from the infirmary were that Mrs Morris was 'going on favourably'.

However, Catherine Morris's injuries were too severe for any permanent improvement and a little over a week later she died. Now the charge was murder.

Philip Morris was 49 at the time of his trial and the drama was played out to a packed courthouse at the Bristol Summer Assizes. The prosecution was represented by Messrs Hooper and Matthews and Mr Norris defended the prisoner.

Mr Hooper opened proceedings by stressing the severity of the case and he prayed for the 'earnest and careful attention' of the jury. He gave a resumé of the prisoner's life, the greater part of which had been spent serving in the army with the Royal Artillery from which he was discharged with a pension in 1870.

The following year he married Catherine who had been married twice before. Her first husband was a man named Thomas Burke whom she wed at Trenchard Street Roman Catholic chapel on 15 November 1840 and had children with, now grown up. Her second marriage, at the same venue, on 12 December 1854 was to a man called Matthew Cahill by whom she had one son, Michael, who was approaching his

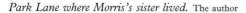

Park Lane where Morris's sister lived. The author

From St Michael's Hill looking towards the city. Watercolour by Colin Downs

tenth birthday at the time of his mother's death. Her wedding to Philip Morris took place at the registry office on 24 April 1871.

One might imagine she thought she had found quite a prize in Philip Morris who was in receipt of an army pension and also earned a wage working as a custom-house officer. She was a skilled tailoress so, on the surface, they should have been able to live quite well. Sadly they both seem to have been addicted to alcohol and by the time the tragedy occurred were living in one room on Narrow Quay for which they paid 2s 6d per week. The state of the room, the dirt and the squalor bore witness to how low they had sunk in their drink-fuelled existence. When the room was searched after the assault over forty pawn tickets were discovered.

Mr Hooper then reiterated the seriousness of the case. He pointed out that the prisoner was 'under the influence of liquor – how far it did not matter, for drunkenness was no excuse for crime'. 'It would be most unreasonable if it were', he explained 'for then drunkards would enjoy a privilege which sober people did not.' To warrant a verdict of manslaughter the jury must be satisfied that there was sufficient provocation to justify him in using the violence of which he was guilty. He told them 'they would hear from his lordship what was deemed sufficient provocation'. As he elaborated the point, defence interrupted quoting 'Cox's Crown Cases' where the issue was 'laid down contrary to my friend's statement'. The judge, Mr Justice Quain, then intervened saying 'The words must be of a very extraordinary character to justify violence'.

Mr Hooper continued in his clarification of the charge saying 'if a man kills another by sudden influence they are not to reduce it to manslaughter if he resorts to a deadly weapon, except that it is in his hand at the time'. He called up the facts of this case, asking what quarrel there had been. He considered that 'no discovery of his wife's misconduct was sufficient to rouse a sudden influence even in the mind of a drunken man'. He referred to Mrs Beckett's evidence given at the earlier hearing and drew the jury's attention to the fact that she heard no violent quarrel which she would have done, living in the room directly above that the Morrises occupied. He conceded that the sound of blows might not have penetrated her room but 'angry expressions delivered in a loud tone' would certainly have done so. He also wanted to examine the surgeon's statement regarding the head injuries inflicted on Mrs Morris. They were consistent with considerable violence. Thus, he felt, the violence used by the prisoner was not such as could possibly be justified.

The first witness to be called for the prosecution was Eliza Burke. She explained she was the wife of Catherine's son Thomas and they lived in Pipe Lane. She said that Catherine Morris had been married twice before she wed Philip Morris 'about 4 or 5 years ago'. She had known the prisoner since the marriage and knew he had been in the army. She said 'He has not done much. His wife used to work hard at the needle. He had lately been at work at the Custom House'. She said that in the past she had usually seen the couple every week and 'sometimes they had a few words'. She denied being present when Catherine Morris exchanged her husband's war medals in a public house, for drink.

Next to be called was Michael Cahill who said he would be '10 next month'. He then proceeded to describe the Morris lifestyle and the day in question saying he slept at the house the night before the 5th; and also: 'Prisoner and mother also slept there. There were two beds in the room. On Monday morning Mother went for some whisky. She went three times.' He went on to say that she bought half a pint on each occasion, going out at 7 o'clock for the first time. She and her husband sat in bed drinking it. Then at about 9 o'clock he was sent out for some and fetched 'a noggin' at his stepfather's behest. He remembered a Mrs Duggin coming to call and she had some of the whisky. At that point, about 9.30, young Michael went out to play, not returning until about 1.30. He had not seen either his mother or stepfather in the hours between but when he did return his mother was lying on the bed, bleeding. 'There was blood on the foot of the bed' the little lad recalled, 'and on my bed and on the wall. I spoke to her and she said something to me. I called in Mrs Price.'

He went on to explain that his mother worked as a tailor and used a sleeve board which she kept against the window. When he returned that Monday lunchtime it was on his bed. He said that before he left the house 'Father and Mother seemed good humoured. I heard no quarrelling'.

Under cross-examination he told the court that it was not a very large room where he slept and there was just one window in it. The bed where his parents slept was away from the window and his bed was on the other side. His mother used the board every day and when she had finished her work it was put away under the window. He said his mother never sent him to pawn things and he could not remember telling the magistrates that she had. On being pressed on this point he said he knew what 'pawning' was and admitted that he had been sent out once but the second time he went the pawnbroker refused him. He then said his mother had pawned trousers and shirts. On being questioned about fetching the whisky on the fateful morning he said he frequently was sent with the jar and brought it back half full. He used to get six-pennyworth from the Assembly Rooms.

It was then Mrs Duggin's turn to face Mr Matthews. She said she lived at 1 Mill Avenue, Queen Square and that on 5 April she went to the prisoner's house and saw him there with his wife. They were in bed at the time but no incident occurred during her time there, neither were they drinking when she arrived but while she was there 'the little boy brought in a noggin of whisky'. She said Morris appeared to have been drinking but she could not say what state his wife was in and barely stayed 5 minutes. They were alone when she left and seemed in good spirits.

Mary Ann Lamb was called next. She said she was 11 years old and her stepfather, a man with the surname Gory, owned the house where Morris occupied one room. She told how she went to collect the rent at about 11 o'clock but could get no reply to her knock so called on Mrs Beckett first, then returned to the Morris's door. This time Morris told her to come in. He and Mrs Morrises' were in bed although Mrs Morris was dressed. On being asked how much rent was owed Mary Ann replied '4 months' and Morris seemed astonished. He asked his wife what made her owe 4 months and she asked him what made him owe it. He asked her what she did with the money and she asked him the same. The girl said that Mrs Morris usually paid her – usually on a monthly basis but this time she had 'been for the rent a good many times' and had even accosted Morris on the quay the preceding Saturday at midday and he had promised they would bring it down that afternoon.

After this debate Sarah Beckett glanced out of her window and saw Morris go down the lane. He appeared to be very tipsy. About 5 minutes later he returned but Sarah heard nothing from the room below until Michael came home and then Mrs Morris being taken away to the infirmary by the police. She confessed that she had often seen her intoxicated and knew she pawned things, including 'a suit of clothes I entrusted her to make'. She was then questioned about the pawning of Morris's medals but said she knew nothing about that but could remember her throwing a bottle at him causing quite a severe injury a couple of months before. She knew Morris had been to the police once or twice to complain about her behaviour.

Another of the residents, Elizabeth Price, was questioned. She and her husband Edwin occupied the room directly opposite that of the Morrises. She explained she had gone out about 9.30 on that morning and returned about 10.40 at which time she met Morris on the stairs and he stood aside for her to pass. She left her door open and she saw him return to his room within a few moments and shut the door. Some 5 minutes later he quitted the room again. She heard nothing then until Michael came to her room for help. She described how she found Mrs Morris lying on the bed covered in blood. On being asked about Mrs Morris's habit of pawning possessions she admitted she had 'once or twice pawned things' for her. She was aware the couple often had arguments.

PC Capper then described the arrest which was made at his sister's home in Park Lane, at the back of St Michael's church. She cried and said to him 'Oh Philip, why did you live with that wretch?' to which he replied 'It is no use crying now; it's done and can't be helped. I told you it would come to this. I told you I would be hanged for her.' On the way to the police station he continued to bemoan his dismal marriage and was asked 'Why did you live with her?' He also said 'How could I get away from the wretch?'

Morris's unblemished military career was cited in his favour at the trial. He possessed four good conduct badges, the Crimean Medal with three clasps and the Turkish War Medal. His defending counsel asked the jury to consider this and the fact that the accused had fallen into habits of intemperance due to the 'evil life led by the deceased woman'. Colonel Alexander McLean, staff officer of pensioners in the district averred that he had always found him a 'well-conducted man' and had sufficient confidence in him to employ him in his own house. Mr T H Fisher, custom house officer, had employed him since 1872 and said he was 'so well conducted a man that he was promoted from an ordinary to a preferable extra man. He was a most inoffensive man'.

It was mooted that perhaps the charge could be reduced to manslaughter but the jury, after retiring for a mere 15 minutes,

returned a verdict of wilful murder but with a strong recommendation to mercy on account of his former good conduct.

The judge then assumed the black cap and passed sentence
although the words he spoke were tinged with regret and Morris
walked firmly from the dock.

Within a couple of weeks a petition for reprieve had been
signed by 14,230 people. All the members of the jury had
signed apart from one who was in Ireland but even he sent a
telegraph saying how glad he would have been to append his
signature. The letter, conveyed to London, begged the recipient
to 'save the poor fellow's life who, from having such a dreadful
partner, was riven when excited by drink, to commit the crime
which in his sober moments would have been furthermost from
his mind'. It was signed by J A Gardner, governor of Bristol City
Gaol.

The reprieve was granted. The news was conveyed to the
prisoner early on a Saturday morning and he received the
tidings 'with deep emotion but managed to preserve a proper
demeanour while the governor was addressing him'. On being
given a prayer book he sat down at the table in his cell and
offered up a prayer. Apparently he had initially kept up 'a very
firm demeanour' but the stress of waiting to hear whether or not
he would be hanged had, not surprisingly, begun to tell on him
latterly. After a couple of weeks he was moved to Pentonville
from whence he would be shipped to one of the colonies for a
lifetime of penal servitude. A grim fate, without a doubt but
better than the alternative and one hopes, perhaps, that at some
stage he gained remission and a few years of freedom in some
foreign land.

CHAPTER 9

Charlotte's Concealment
1875

... she was horrified to see the body of a child lying there.

The year was 1875 and spring had arrived on the slopes of Ashley Down. It is difficult to imagine nowadays how the scene would have appeared in those days before the housing estates of Horfield and Lockleaze came into being; when the future Muller Road was a rambling lane meandering across pastureland down towards the River Frome which flooded at regular intervals.

The hillside was dotted with farms, barns and cottages, while further down were apple orchards and market gardens in the shadow of the woodlands which clustered on Purdown, dominating the view and surrounding Heath House, one of the homes of Sir John Smythe and, in fact, the one in which he chose to live. The lane leading to the entrance still bears his name today.

A glance at the local paper, the *Bristol Times and Mirror*, revealed vital information for the fashion-conscious females of the city as materials in 'every colour and style' were flooding into Bristol that spring. Checked materials were especially popular with 'the prettiest style' using a design of checks in contrasting shades such as café au lait and chestnut or light blue on dark. The Parisienne influence was strong with delicate Pompadour foulards stealing the show, pink moss roses, blue beribboned on a white background being a favourite choice.

It is to be doubted that Mary Ann Gingell was too concerned about whether or not the 'Marie Antionette' would be more popular than the 'Printemps' in the coming season as she walked across the grass to gather some violets to place round the well on the land behind her home to which her family had more or less exclusive use. She and her husband, Daniel, a farm labourer, had lived in a house adjoining Ashley Down for 2 years.

There had been a change in their domestic arrangements a few months previously which had caused a little unrest. Daniel's sister, Charlotte, had arrived on the scene at Christmas with her two children aged eight and three.

It is not known what explanation she gave for her flight from Lullington on the Wiltshire–Somerset border where she had lived formerly but there were a number of unexplained features of Charlotte's life.

She called herself Charlotte Morris but no trace of a husband past or present had ever been verified. She quickly settled into a small room in Daniel's house where the only furniture was a box and a bed, no bedstead. There was little privacy as Mary Ann and Daniel had to use the room to gain access to their own bedroom but this seemed not to concern Charlotte. Soon after she arrived she managed to procure work as a washerwoman.

Before long a communication was sent to the Gingells from Lullington to advise them that Charlotte was 'in the family way'. They tackled Charlotte with this accusation telling her that, if there was any truth in the rumour then she had better take her children and go elsewhere. Charlotte, however, strenuously denied the charge and swore solemn oaths that it was all a terrible lie. She was so convincing that Mary Ann believed her absolutely.

So life continued in the house near Ashley Down with Charlotte going off to work each day and often not returning until late each night.

This, then, was the situation on that day in late March, Easter Tuesday, when, around midday, Mary Ann walked across the field behind her house, the meadow they called Russell's Fields, to gather violets to place round the well. Their own supply of soft water had run very low so her purpose was to draw some from the well which had not been used since the summer before. She tied a rope to her bucket and raised the well cover. Then, as she glanced down to see the level of the water, she was horrified to see the body of a child lying there.

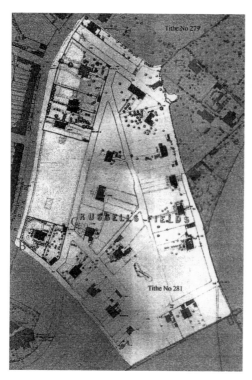

*A tithe map showing Russell's Fields.
That part marked 'A' is where
Neville Road was later built.
'B' indicates Wesley Road and
'C' the site of Brynland Avenue.*
Reproduced courtesy of Denis Wright,
extracted from *Population in Horfield
1066–1851*

She ran to the police station and fetched Acting-Sergeant
Critchley who returned with her to the house. He managed to
raise the body from the well and carried it away, watched by a
group of women who had gathered there. Among them was
Charlotte Morris. He then asked Mary Ann if she could find
something in which he could wrap the child and she went into
the kitchen and brought him a piece of torn green apron she had
found there. On being asked to whom it belonged she said 'My
sister-in-law'.

As the policeman unwrapped it he noticed some marks on
the material and asked Charlotte what they were to which she
replied 'I didn't use that with the child'. He then told her he
was going to take her into custody on a charge of concealment
of birth. Charlotte, who had a slab of butter in her hand said
'Well, let me go into the house with this,' and she turned
towards the kitchen door but Critchley was close behind her
and saw her place the butter on the table and snatch at a knife

lying there. He grabbed her wrist and forced her to drop it and asked her what she intended doing with it. 'Oh, I was not going to hurt you,' she protested and he said 'But you probably would yourself.' With this he pulled her away from the table.

She began to resist then and said she would not be taken and became extremely agitated so that he had to carry her out by force although she calmed down considerably by the time they reached the police station.

Once she was in custody he returned to the Gingells' house and carried out a thorough search in company with Superintendent Rawle. It was not the first time he had searched the house since Charlotte took up residence there. On 7 January that year he had checked the property having been given to believe that there were stolen goods on the premises. Charlotte had answered the door to him then and he had been certain that she was pregnant.

Meanwhile, Mary Ann and her mother had found some bloodstained clothing and bedding, also part of an apron pushed under the oven. Any other materials that had been besmirched with blood had been spirited away from the house as Charlotte always took her washing to work and combined it with the laundry for which she was paid to deal. The pebbles around the well were also found to be covered in bloodstains.

Wesley Road in present times. Author's collection

Brynland Avenue as it is today. Author's collection

Robert Fendick, MRCS was called in by the police to examine both the body of the child and Charlotte Morris. He gave the opinion that Charlotte had been confined during the last 2 to 3 days.

He then turned his attention to the baby girl, a full-grown, well-developed child. He found some marks of discolouration on the eyelids but no signs of external violence. The umbilical cord had been severed with a blunt instrument and torn. Examination of the lungs showed that the lungs had inflated and he found the right cavity of the heart full of partly coagulated blood, the left totally empty. All these findings led him to the conclusion the child had been alive at birth and its death was caused by drowning. The naked baby had been immersed in about 4 feet of water at the bottom of the 12-foot well.

The inquest was held at the *Horfield Inn* under the jurisdiction of Dr E M Grace, the West Gloucestershire coroner. When the accused was brought into the room she was asked by

New Road, Eastville,

The building of Muller Road in the 1920s which marked the end of the rural aspect of the area. Pamela Fursman collection

him if she wished to be present at the enquiry to which she responded 'Yes, I shouldn't mind stopping'.

Charlotte was 33 years old at the time and described as having a 'strong, hardy appearance'. It is reported she seemed little concerned with the proceedings and frequently laughed during the enquiry.

She appeared before the magistrates at Lawford's Gate the following day when virtually the same evidence was produced and a verdict of 'Wilful Murder' was brought against the prisoner as she was committed for trial on the capital charge.

She was tried at the Gloucester Assizes where the evidence was once again presented although one piece of information emerged which had previously been undisclosed. It transpired that Charlotte Morris, *alias* Gingell, had, in fact, given birth to eight illegitimate children in the course of her adult life. It is, then, perhaps puzzling that she decided this child had to die. Was she trying to retrieve her reputation at this late stage in her life?

Charlotte Morris was sentenced to 18 months' imprisonment with hard labour, a small price, one might think, for sacrificing a baby girl's life.

Chapter 10

A Dangerous Liaison
1880

You have stabbed me.

In 1880 Jane Gillard occupied a house in Wellington Road, St Paul's which ran parallel to Newfoundland Road. Later the road extended to include what was then the Rope Walk. At the time of the incident it was just a terrace of houses fronting on to the river.

Mrs Gillard had settled down for the night when one of her lodgers, a woman she knew as Mrs Eliza Distin, stumbled in. She was in a distraught state and was bleeding profusely from a wound in her left shoulder.

She cried 'He have stabbed me. He have done it again. Go and see what he is doing'. She then staggered back to her own room with Jane Gillard in her wake.

The attacker, William Distin, usually, it appears, known as Joe, was later described as being in 'a stupid state'. By this time Eliza was collapsing and Mrs Gillard screamed at him 'You have stabbed your wife and she is dying. What have you done, you villain?'. As Eliza sank to the floor Distin rose from his chair and advanced towards the injured woman saying 'Eliza, dear, what have I done? What is the matter?' to which she replied, 'You have stabbed me. You have done for me this time.'

Mrs Gillard, concerned at the amount of blood Eliza was losing, ordered Distin to fetch a doctor but when he put on his hat and coat Eliza said 'You want to go away now you have done it, but you must not'. With this Jane Gillard ran downstairs and fetched George Tilling, landlord of the *Holly Branch* tavern, also in Wellington Road, who brought a friend along. Also present was Mrs Emma Bave, a shoemaker's wife from number 8. When Mr Tilling saw the extent of Eliza's injuries

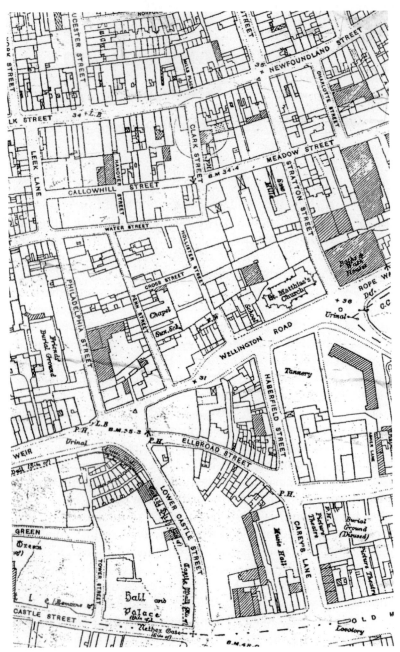

A map of the area where the crime took place showing both Wellington Road and Philadelphia Street. Author's collection

The last remnants of Wellington Road pictured in 2006. The Phoenix *is the sole pub remaining occupied here.* The author

he sent his pal to fetch a policeman and tried to staunch the flow of blood by means of applying wet rags to the wound. He found a bloodstained knife on the floor near where the woman lay. He demanded of Distin 'What made you do this?' and was told 'Oh, through jealousy'. Eliza was clearly alarmed when she realised there was going to be police involvement. She said 'Oh, don't fetch a policeman; let me lie and die happy'.

Her wish was not to be granted for the police arrived as she spoke. PC John Payne from nearby Trinity Road police station arrived with another officer and George Tilling handed over one bloodstained knife and Emma Bave produced another, also covered in blood which she said had been on the table.

PC Payne informed Distin that they would have to take him into custody at which stage he became very aggressive and swore at them saying that it would take a better man than Payne to do so and he kicked the officer. When he eventually arrived at the police station he exhibited another show of violence. He was clearly intoxicated and pretended to know nothing of the offence on which he was being charged. He was remanded in custody for a week.

Meanwhile, the police built up their case and pieced together the events leading up to the events of that evening, 27 September 1880.

Eliza's name was not, in fact, Distin but Daniels and her life had been far from ordinary. Born Emily Eliza Tamlin, she had been married to a steward of an ocean-going steamer and she had sometimes travelled with him as a stewardess. Her husband had died in China in 1866 and she had returned to Bristol and had helped her sister run a public house. For whatever reason she changed careers and became a nurse at the Bristol Royal Infirmary but after about a year she decided to return to working as a stewardess on a route between England and America. Eventually she decided her travelling days were over and she took up residence with her mother. It was while she was living there that her path disastrously crossed that of William Distin. He persuaded her to move in with him and pass herself off as his wife. In August 1879 she moved in with him. Her new home was in Philadelphia Street, a thoroughfare which ran from Broad Weir to Water Street and was demolished for the re-development of Broadmead in the 1950s–1960s. Thirty-six-year-old Distin was a cabinet maker by trade. He was employed by a Mr Payne whose workshop was in Castle Ditch. Eliza, who was 39, was said to be 'devotedly attached to him' despite the fact their relationship seems to have been a stormy one. They had moved the short distance to Wellington Road, where they occupied a single room, a week before the attack. There was a reason for this, of which more later.

On the day in question, Monday 27 September, Distin appears to have decided he had had enough of work for the day and persuaded a young workmate, one George Ferris, to go to a pub with him. At a little after 1 o'clock they repaired to the *Old Castle*. At 5.15 Eliza went to his workplace, discovered he was not there and went to find him. There was later some dispute as to what was said when she did catch up with him although, at the time, young George said 'no angry words passed between them'. They sat down together and had a glass of beer but it was noted that, while Distin was not drunk, he was certainly 'the worse for liquor'. They stayed in the pub, with George Ferris, until 8.45 when they all walked back to the house in Wellington

Church Lane, Temple, location of Distin's family home. Watercolour by Colin Downs

Road and had some supper. They had brought back a quart of beer which they shared and when George Ferris left them he said they were 'perfectly good friends'.

So what happened to cause the outbreak of violence?

As it transpired, Distin had a long history of aggressive behaviour and alcoholism caused by, if his counsel at the trial was to be believed, a severe blow to the head when he was working as an apprentice. Over the years he had made eight or nine suicide attempts. He had numerous convictions for being drunk and disorderly and as far back as 1866 he had been bound over for 'violently assaulting his father'. In June 1870 he had tried to kill himself by taking a quantity of 'Hunter's Vermin and Insect Destroying Powder' at his father's house in Church Lane, Temple. He was treated at the General Hospital. In September 1872 he was charged with being drunk and disorderly and fighting in Rosemary Street and committed a similar offence in Corn Street 2 months later. At his trial this behaviour was blamed on a head injury and sunstroke he had suffered while young for, it was said, his early years were full of promise and he was a gifted musician when, while attending the Counterslip school, he was billed as 'The Distin Prodigy' performing as one of 'Dr Mark's Little Men'.

By 1873 he was becoming more antagonistic towards the police and, as well as being drunk and disorderly he was also charged with resisting arrest and assaulting the police. By the September of that year his behaviour seems to have spiralled out of control and he was imprisoned for 21 days, with hard labour, for attacking his mother, Maria, and assaulting the police who came to arrest him. The experience did nothing to curb his vicious nature or his dependence on alcohol for, on 11 November, he was again arrested for being drunk, assaulting his mother and Elizabeth Brown and attacking the police when they arrived on the scene. This time he had to serve 3 months in gaol, again with hard labour. A little over a month after his release he was back inside again following a drunken show of violence towards his sister Emily.

In 1876 he received another three-month sentence for destroying pictures and ornaments at 2 Church Lane, the property of his long-suffering mother. This time another sister,

Rose, bore the brunt of his drunken rage. His life was a series of attacks and arrests, all the incidents being drink-fuelled and most of his aggression seems to have been directed at his family.

In May 1880, by which time he was co-habiting with Eliza, his behaviour had become more extreme and he was arrested for being 'drunk and disorderly and exposing his naked person in Temple Street'. A little over a month later he was committed to prison for 'unlawfully cutting and wounding Eliza Daniels at 25 Philadelphia Street by stabbing her in the face with a knife with intent to do her grievous bodily harm'. This may well be why the pair had to seek alternative accommodation when he was released.

And then, in September 1880, came the final assault. After Eliza was admitted to the infirmary, where once she had worked as a nurse, the surgeon found a deep wound which began in the upper part of the arm and passed through the muscles connecting the chest with the shoulder and 'was turned by a large vein under the collar bone'. It was from this large vein that the rush of blood emanated. At first doctors were hopeful that she would make a full recovery but, sadly, an injury had been done to the covering of the lungs and inflammation there led to an infection causing her to go downhill fast. On 14 October a deposition was taken. Initially she had insisted it was an accident but when it was read back to her she said 'How can I say it was an accident?'. She died on 16 October.

Meanwhile William Joseph Distin had been remanded in custody. Now he had to face the magisterial enquiry and the inquest.

The whole process was somewhat drawn out as a post-mortem had to be held and several adjournments had to be made.

At the inquest, which was held at the infirmary, the first to be called was Eliza's mother, Sarah Tamlin, who lived in Tucker Street which ran off the Rope Walk. She stated that after the incident in June when Distin had attacked Eliza she had begged her daughter to leave him, offering her food and shelter but Eliza would not be swayed. The clerk to the magistrates, who had taken down the dying woman's deposition which she had given in front to Distin. During the procedure Distin had challenged her, accusing her of cutting him above one eye but Eliza had averred 'I had not the heart to hurt a human being, certainly not you'. Her version of the events on the fateful night were that they had been in a pub on the Rope Walk and that several persons 'sat down to supper' with them. She admitted that when he had partaken of too much liquor he had difficulty remembering what events had taken place.

At the hearings Distin was voluble when he disagreed with witness statements. He challenged Eliza's mental state at the time she made her deposition saying 'I say she was not right when that evidence was taken. A woman in her right mind would never ask for tea at such times as that'.

He became extremely hot under the collar when Thirza Bryant, their former landlady, was being cross-examined. She is described as being 'the wife of a labourer, living at 25 Phila-delphia Street'. She testified that the couple had quarrelled frequently when they had been drinking and mentioned the previous occasion when Distin had attacked Eliza. He began to shout at her, saying 'You're a liar. Don't you stand there and tell such **** lies. You were the one that set her on; you were the one that got her to go and drink and come home and abuse me, and you were the one that struck me and cut my head open you **** ****. You told her to go out on the streets and bring you the money'. The usher then tried to calm him down but Distin refused to be halted. 'Everyone in the street knows what she is' he declared. 'I owe her 2 or 3 shillings and because she won't get it she comes against me, I suppose.'

On being advised that he was only making things worse for himself he retorted 'It don't trouble me. There's nothing like having your name in the newspapers and giving them some-thing worth the penny. It makes the paper sell better'. He con-tinued to contradict every word Thirza Bryant uttered insisting 'It was through her beautiful daughter the row happened', and I think we are to assume the adjective was used in an ironic sense.

And so it went on, Thirza doggedly giving her evidence, Distin refuting every word, referring to her as 'the nuisance of Philadelphia Street' and taunting her with the words 'I suppose you're going to have a bob for this lot. It'll buy you a pint of rum at the *King Billy* in Philadelphia Street. Oh! She can look fearful and she's had part of my wages many a time'.

Thirza described the earlier attack when 'there was blood all over the place. The prisoner was on top of the woman and had almost strangled her, her being black in the face'. She said he had said many times that he would never be happy until he had killed her, adding that the children had heard his threats. The mention of the children brought forth another rash of venom 'it's a pretty lot from the youngest to the oldest'; and he shouted 'That woman swears and drinks and yet she pretends to go to mothers' meetings. What does she get there? Why, tea and snacks'.

When asked if he wanted to question her he retorted: 'Me! Do you think I'm mad?' to which the rejoinder came from the witness 'You're not right' and a slanging match ensued in which sarcastic reference to Thirza's attendance at St Barnabas church.

Distin was then committed for trial at the Gloucester Assizes.

He was represented by a Mr Valpry who was to struggle to counter the prosecution's case set out by Messrs Hooper and Poole. The account of the day's events leading up to the assault varied little from the inquest evidence although one incident which was mentioned only in passing previously was used by the defence in a vain attempt to explain Distin's actions. As will be remembered, two knives were found in the room on the night in question. Valpry pointed out that Eliza had admitted she often used a knife to cut sticks for the fire and his suggestion was that was the explanation for the stabbing – seeing her struggling with the wood he went forward with a knife in his hand in an attempt to help her but being very drunk he stumbled and the knife entered her shoulder.

Much of the earlier evidence relating to past misdemeanours was ruled as inadmissible and so Thirza Bryant's account of the incident in June and her comments on his treatment of Eliza were cut short.

Mr Justice Denman then summed up, emphasising that committing such a brutal act under the influence of drink was no reason to absolve the man. He said 'It was no more a defence for him to say that he was at the time drunk, as long as he had the mind to do these things, than if he was to say that he was a man whose name began with John or anything of that nature'.

The jury were out only for a period of 25 minutes and returned a verdict of guilty of wilful murder with a recommendation to mercy on the grounds that they did not believe it was premeditated. Distin was asked if he had anything to say but did not answer. The judge, donning the black cap, ignored the plea for mercy. Although Distin's previous history had been ruled as inadmissible it clearly influenced the judge. He pronounced the death sentence, urging Distin to spend what time was left to him 'repenting of his conduct'. Distin is reported to having 'walked firmly from the dock'.

The execution took place on 22 November 1880 and a gallows was erected on a lawn on the west side of the gaol 'at a point between Cumberland Road and the Floating Harbour', the first hanging there for 4 years. It seemed he was penitent and stoical during his last days on earth although his fortitude forsook him at the end and, ironically, 'It was found necessary to administer a stimulant'. Death was instantaneous and the black flag was raised at 8.04, for the benefit of the crowd, including women and children, shivering by the river bank.

CHAPTER 11

The Riddle of Richard Rugman
1887

... they heard the latch on the kitchen door click ...

It would seem that Gloucestershire was deemed a particularly dangerous place to live in the 1880s if the local papers are to be believed. Under the headline 'Brutal Murder near Thornbury' it announced that the county had again been 'brought into notoriety by the commission of another murder equalling in daring and nearly surpassing in brutality one or two other outrages that have occurred within the past 18 months'.

This particular crime took place in a tiny hamlet called Morton and the victim was a man of 80 by the name of Richard Rugman. His housekeeper, Miss Eliza Smith, who was 76, was also beaten to within an inch of her life.

The April day in 1887, just prior to the Easter weekend, had been the usual sort of Thursday with a neighbour, Mrs Brown, calling in late afternoon for a chat, leaving them at around 6 o'clock to return to her own home. Another neighbour, James French, called in shortly afterwards and remained in conversation with them until a little after 7 o'clock.

Mr Rugman was sitting in his usual place by the kitchen fire and Miss Smith was seated on a settle nearby when they heard the latch on the kitchen door click and a man appeared in the room, looming over Mr Rugman and demanding he hand over £5. Miss Smith intervened at this point saying: 'My good man, we've got no money to give you, we can't afford it.'

The man, stated later by Miss Smith as being a total stranger to them, became extremely aggressive at her words and began to attack Mr Rugman with a large stick then turning to her and striking her as well. The attack seemed little less than frenzied and the elderly couple were left lying on the floor where they remained in an unconscious state until the following morning when Miss Smith regained sufficient strength to crawl out of the front door and into the garden where she was discovered a little after nine by George Trayburn, a Thornbury trader who was calling to take their meat order.

With the help of a man called Horsman who was working nearby, Trayburn managed to carry the badly disfigured woman into the house where Mr Rugman was found lying on the floor, his head under the settle, still unconscious and having lost a great deal of blood.

Someone went to fetch a doctor and the police and everything possible was done to aid poor Mr Rugman but the prospect of his survival did not look hopeful as his injuries were appalling. He had five or six long wounds to the head and a terrible cut over the left eye and the whole of his face was covered in bruises. His arm, with which he had attempted to protect his head, was broken above the wrist. The hat he always wore was completely smashed, the blows having broken right through the crown and the front part of the brim had, curiously enough, been cut cleanly away leading police to wonder if the bill-hook found in front of the house might have been used in the attack, although a heavy stick nearby had clearly dealt most of the blows.

Eliza Smith, too, was lucky to survive. She had been badly beaten, most of the force being directed at the left side of her body and her face was virtually unrecognisable with the right eye black and closed and a wound on top of her head.

In the room itself were bloodstains over the clock case, the bellows and the mantelpiece.

The horrific incident shocked the local people to the core. Rugman and Eliza had always lived in the area and were known to everyone for miles around. Many years ago they had both been servants but had determined to improve their lot and both of them had put aside part of their wages each week until, nearly

Some present day views of Morton, near Thornbury where Richard Rugman died following a vicious attack in 1887. The author

40 years ago, Rugman had rented a small farm, Eliza putting her savings into the venture as well. As time went by they both made wills leaving everything to the survivor.

After 29 years they decided to give up the farm and retire as Rugman had purchased a cottage years ago while still in service and a man called George Ball took over the farm.

Apparently, Richard Rugman was a cheerful and popular man and was loved by all the local children who always ran to greet him when he passed by although latterly chronic rheumatism had prevented him going out much and he could only walk with the aid of crutches. He had family living in the vicinity, a sister and three brothers, one of whom was 90.

After the attack a bed was made up for him in the kitchen and he was able to recognise the many people who came to see him, including a niece who lived fairly close by. He repeatedly muttered 'I'm very bad; I'm going to die', and then would lapse back into unconsciousness.

On the Saturday afternoon an old friend of his, by the name of Howell, was sitting by his bed when he suddenly said: 'William, did a man come in and hit me with a stick? I suppose I dreamed it.'

His friend tried to establish what the attacker looked like but Rugman, who was rather deaf, made no reply and soon drifted into unconsciousness again. He finally died on the Tuesday.

The police had found it extremely difficult to piece together any sort of case. Accounts were confused and neither Rugman not Eliza Smith could give a clear picture of events because of the severity of their injuries. Robbery was the obvious motive. Richard Rugman had been to the bank at Thornbury on the day in question and it was known throughout the neighbourhood that he had provided comfortably for his old age over the years. However, this sort of knowledge pointed to someone in the neighbourhood familiar with Rugman's affairs and habits and no supporting evidence backed up this theory.

To the best of Eliza's memory the intruder had only been in the house about 10 minutes and she did not believe he had gone up the kitchen stairs to her bedroom where £15 had been left in view on a table. Neither did she recall him searching Rugman's pockets although they were found empty. It was thought that the man, frightened by his own violence, had fled the scene empty handed.

On the Sunday word reached Sergeant Eyles that a man had left the town in the company of two others and that his shirt sleeve was spattered with blood. Taking a trap and accompanied by constables Hemmings and Pledger, he set off in pursuit and caught up with the group at Berkeley. The man, when accosted, appeared agitated, perhaps understandably and when his shirt was examined the marks turned out to be red paint. He was a painter by trade and said he had left Bristol the night before.

The belief that the attacker was a local man gathered momentum. It was thought that a stranger would be unaware that anyone but the humblest cottager might be living in the Rugman dwelling as there were no outward trappings to indicate wealth and, inevitably, suspicions were aroused and fingers pointed at certain people in the community. Over a week passed, Richard Rugman was dead and the police were no nearer solving the crime.

Eliza Smith had to be carried in to attend the adjourned inquest, wrapped in blankets and appeared extremely weak but was able to answer the questions put to her intelligibly. She was cautioned by the coroner Dr E M Grace who asked her if she wished to give evidence. She replied: 'I did not do it and I don't know anyone who did.'

After being sworn she gave an account of the Thursday and mentioned the visits of Mrs Brown and Mr French. She said she heard someone at the door between 8 and 9 o'clock as she and Rugman sat opposite each other by the fireside. She got up from her chair to answer the knock but before she could reach the door it opened and a man entered, shutting it behind him. She could not see his face; he had his back to her then walked round the settle and stood before Rugman demanding £5. She realised he had a stick in his hand but did not see him actually strike Rugman because, she said, she was 'so frightened.' He then turned on her and began to deal with her in a like manner. At this stage she thought she must have passed out. All she could remember about the man was that he was tallish and wore a dark coat.

When she came to she found Rugman on the floor and tried to lift him up, without success. She spent the night in the kitchen and remembered little about those hours; and was not sure whether or not she replenished the fire, although she did recollect she should not go to her room and leave Rugman on his own. Because of his infirmities he always slept in the kitchen.

She recalled leaving the house in the morning but by this time her face was so swollen she could hardly see. She remembered letting the fowls out then falling down outside and being carried in by someone whom she thought was the butcher.

She admitted that she usually kept the door locked at night and could not think why she had not done so on this occasion. On being asked about the murder weapon she doubted whether she would recognise it although she had noticed a whitish stick with some 'rind' peeled off in the man's hand when he came into the room. She had been told it was one which had been in the garden of the cottage and picked up by the intruder before entering the cottage.

Susan Brown, who had visited the couple earlier on the fateful Thursday, was then questioned, saying that she had enquired of Eliza on occasion whether she and Rugman ever quarrelled or assaulted one another and remembered Eliza saying that at the time of attack they 'were on as good terms as they were at any time in their lives and no such thoughts entered their heads'. Apparently, Mrs Brown had been helping Eliza after the incident, drawing water for her as she was too weak to do it herself or pour it from the well bucket. She did not believe that Rugman and Eliza ever fought.

Meanwhile, a suspect, a Francis Frederick Ponting, had been apprehended and charged with Rugman's murder after he had made a statement implicating his guilt but it turned out he was a time waster and was nowhere near the scene of the crime on the night in question.

A week later the inquest was resumed and Dr Taylor who had examined the couple after the attack was called and cross-examined. He was asked how he thought Eliza's injuries were produced and gave his opinion that those to the head, collar bone, neck and shoulders were caused by a blunt instrument 'such as the stick produced'. He was then asked if he thought any of them could have been caused by a fall and he replied that the horizontal head wound was very likely caused by a fall but the blow to the collar bone he thought was sustained by direct violence.

He was then asked to speculate as to whether Eliza might have been struck by the deceased with a crutch as he sat opposite her by the fire and the doctor admitted that it was possible, adding 'I should not like to say it is impossible'. He was then quizzed as to Eliza's mental state and said he believed her memory to be affected by the blows administered to her and said: 'I should not place any importance on any statements she made as regarded what happened soon after the injuries.'

Superintendent Critchley, who had taken charge of the case, had made an enquiry about the number of blows she had suffered and Dr Taylor thought at least six or seven. He was then asked by a juror if he thought Eliza could have launched an attack on Richard Rugman after having sustained these injuries and he replied that he did not think she could. The coroner then posed the question: 'Do you believe it possible that Richard Rugman could have inflicted the injuries on her before any injuries were received by him?'

Dr Taylor said he considered it possible he had sufficient strength before he was hurt. As to whether or not Eliza could have made the attack on Rugman before she was hurt the doctor said 'I don't think she could'.

A neighbour from Lower Morton, Ada Howell, was then called. She described how she went to the cottage at about 9 o'clock on Good Friday morning and found both Rugman and Eliza Smith lying on the floor and George Trayburn there. He told her that he had carried Eliza in and placed her in a chair but she had fainted, knocked over the table and slid on to the floor. She noticed that Eliza's hands were covered with blood. Someone drew her attention to the fact that the soap was smeared with blood.

Sergeant Eyles then related his story of being called to the cottage and listening to Eliza Smith's account of the intruder. In the room in which she was found, he said, there was a bureau but none of the drawers had been disturbed although the keys were in the top part and he had searched the bedrooms and had found nothing disturbed there. PC Hemming who had also been called to the scene testified that he had found a purse containing 13 sovereigns and there were 2 half-sovereigns, half a crown and sixpence in another purse. He called on the deceased, he said, every day until the day of his death but he never heard Rugman say anything about a man entering the cottage and attacking him.

Between 8 April and 2 May Eliza Smith had said she had met with some of her 'accidents' by falling down outside the house. She said she remembered perfectly well falling down twice and hurting her shoulders and head and she recollected 'something running down her face'.

Superintendent Critchley said that when he went to the house and saw Eliza Smith there was thick blood on the back of her right hand and there were also two or three grey hairs on it. The back of the left hand was smeared with blood but the palms appeared to have been washed and he drew Sergeant Eyles attention to this fact. He mentioned it to Eliza who said: 'Oh, I didn't know.' Apparently she sank back then and he did not question her further although he did elicit the information that she was certain the intruder did not go into the room where the bureau was, or upstairs.

The coroner then summed up, remarking that obviously the injuries which led to Richard Rugman's death were not self inflicted and they had to consider what reason would lead to anyone going to the house to beat two old people. There must have been some motive – either robbery or revenge and if that was the case was it likely they would have gone without carrying some weapon with them and it had been established the stick used was one which had already been in Rugman's garden. He asked the jury to consider the height of the kitchen and consider whether it was possible for a man to stand up and deliver the blows as Eliza had described. They must either accept her evidence or disregard it entirely. He pointed out that Dr Taylor had said Eliza did not have the strength to administer the blows but they had to consider whether she could have done it when he was lying on the floor. If the jury believed that an intruder had entered the cottage and committed the crime then the verdict had to be wilful murder but if they decided Eliza and Rugman had quarrelled then the charge would be manslaughter because they would not consider in an ordinary way that Eliza Smith, using that stick, would be able to murder Richard Rugman.

The room was cleared at 8.45 to allow the jury to consider their verdict and an hour later they returned one of 'Wilful murder against some person or persons unknown'.

So Eliza was given the benefit of the doubt. But what really happened in that firelit kitchen on the night before Good Friday in 1887? Did the elderly couple have a violent argument which led to such a vicious conclusion that one of them died? Did Eliza concoct her story to cover up the true facts? Or did a passing stranger, perhaps someone who had kept a watch on the house and thought he would chance his luck, come in, make his demands then launch an attack through frustration in meeting resistance from a couple of old people, who refused to hand over their hard-earned cash to some 'chancer'?

Alas, after all these years, we shall never know the truth.

CHAPTER 12

A Convoluted Case
1889

...Jane was lying on the bed with blood flowing from her nose and mouth.

Today the St Philips area of Bristol is mainly industrial with just small pockets of houses as a reminder of how things might have looked in past times. In 1889 when the Withey case took place the district was densely populated with row upon row of terraced dwellings with front doors opening directly on to the street.

The residential properties were peppered with countless little shops, off-licences and pubs and the close proximity of neighbours seemed to breed a strong community spirit. It is this brand of loyalty which figures strongly in the death of Jane Withey and its aftermath.

Jane Withey was 36 years of age in 1889 and lived with her husband John at 21 Cumberland Street together with their four children, Frederick, Alfred, Sarah and Emily whose ages ranged from 10 to 16. John, 2 years older than his wife, worked as a stoker at the local gas works where he had been employed for 11 years. He also had a side-line – slaughtering animals for local butchers. In spite of this additional revenue they still lived in virtual penury, the entire family inhabiting two small rooms. The bedroom was about 12-foot square and the parents occupied a 3-foot bed in the centre while the children slept on bundles of rags in the corners of the room.

Life had not always been like this for the Witheys. At one time John was running a small shop but in latter years had taken to drink. Jane also had this failing, being described as 'given

Cumberland Street where the Withey family lived. Collection of the late Benjamin Price

away very much to drink, so much so that she was hardly ever out of a public house'.

So this, then, was the situation in February 1889 when Bristol first read about what the *Bristol Times and Mirror* referred to as 'The St Philips Mystery'.

It is said that on 11 February, a Monday, 'nothing particular appeared to have occurred until the evening'. It would seem the first incident which could have presaged trouble ahead was between 6 and 7 o'clock when Jane Withey encountered next door neighbour Alice Bartlett. Alice noted that Jane had been drinking. They parted at the door of number 21. A short while afterwards Annie Sainsbury from number 18 passed the house and the door was open. Jane was sitting by the fire. She called Annie in and confided to her that she had spent the rent money and was going to bed 'to get myself square by the time Jack comes in'. Annie was later to testify that Jane had clearly been drinking.

It is at this juncture that certain inconsistencies arose in depositions made following the tragedy but it was generally conceded that the most likely sequence of events was thus. John Withey arrived home from work between 6.00 and 7.00 and sent one of the girls out to get him some supper. Then a few words were exchanged between the couple on the subject of Jane squandering all the money John had given her on Saturday so that there was nothing left to pay the rent. The youngsters agreed that both parents were cross and irritable and that John Withey had ordered them all to bed at about 7.30. It was suggested this was to avoid the landlord who was due to call at 8 o'clock.

The Star Inn, Sussex Street *which, due to its proximity to Cumberland Street, was doubtless one of Jane Withey's ports of call.* Lewis Wilshire collection

It is hard to imagine how the next couple of hours were spent cooped up in that little room. What is known is that 10-year-old Emily Kate was despatched to Taylor's bakery on the corner of Sussex Street and Edward Street. According to Mrs Charlotte Taylor, the baker's wife, the little girl bought a loaf of bread at 10 o'clock. Emily stated she went straight back to bed on her return and did not know whether or not her mother ate her supper. If this is true events must have happened swiftly after that because at 10.30 neighbours were alerted by screams of 'murder' emanating from number 21.

Frederick said that it was he who raised the alarm. He could not say what woke him. In court he was to swear that he heard no scream. He simply woke up and went to his mother's side of the bed where a lamp was left burning on the mantelshelf as he and his brother and the father had to get up early to go to work. He noticed his mother was lying back on the bed with blood

All that remains of Sussex Street today. The author

flowing from her nose and mouth. He stated that he then went round to the other side of the bed where his father was snoring loudly and it took him 3 or 4 minutes to wake him up. When John was apprised of the dire situation 'he made a great outcry and woke up the other children'. Later, Sarah Ann was to state that when she looked at her mother she noticed that the bedclothes were pulled down below her waist and there was blood flowing from her left side. For some unexplained reason John Withey, on being given the news regarding his wife, immediately took himself off downstairs. Almost immediately Alice Bartlett appeared on the scene, wondering what on earth was happening. The front door did not close properly and a piece of furniture was jammed against it at night. When she was eventually able to enter the house Withey told her that his wife was dead. She went straight up to the bedroom where, she was subsequently to aver, Jane was lying on the bed with blood flowing from her nose and mouth. The bedclothes were pulled up to her chin.

The sequence of events after this point is somewhat hazy. Certainly another neighbour, Mrs Elizabeth Nutt, entered the house shortly after Alice Bartlett and they were soon joined by a

Mrs Crinks, Sophie Tarrant and Ellen Williams – both from nearby Barter's Buildings, George Lane – Mrs Moss and several other local women. Apparently they tried to revive her with brandy but she was beyond human help by this time. Even more neighbours had congregated outside the house and had attracted the notice of PC Hiscocks, who overheard someone say 'Fetch a policeman'. He walked into the kitchen of number 21 and found Withey sitting there. On being questioned by the policeman Withey said his wife had burst a blood vessel. He denied having quarrelled with his wife and said he had been in bed since 7 o'clock. He was fully dressed but the children and neighbours testified that often, when he was the worse for drink, he would go to bed removing only his scarf, jacket and boots. The officer went upstairs to what must have been an extremely crowded bedroom and was told by Alfred that there had been no quarrel between his parents that night. On being asked what had alerted him to his wife's condition Withey replied 'She screamed out'. When it was queried why he had not sent for the doctor he made no direct reply but asked the constable if he would fetch medical aid. In the end one of the boys was despatched to fetch the surgeon, Mr Page, from Old Market Street. Apparently he arrived at the house at about 11.30 when he was told by the women assembled there that Mrs Withey had died of a broken blood vessel and that a policeman had been

Midland Road as it would have looked in 1889. Grace Cooper collection

called in. When he was asked his opinion he declined to give one until a post-mortem had taken place at which time he said he would issue a death certificate. He did not examine the body of this 'well nourished woman' – her weight was given variously as between 12 and 13 stone and between 14 and 16 stone – until 13 February.

It was later said that it was while the doctor was present in the house that John Withey threatened to do away with himself but Alfred had already taken three knives next door to the Bartlett household by this time if George Bartlett's evidence is to be given credence. Apparently Alfred's reason for this action was to prevent his father attempting suicide. He was to say that he found the knife beside his mother in the bed. He took it down to show his father and that is when the suicide threats were made.

The following morning at 9.00 John Withey, accompanied by Mrs Nutt, called at St Philips police station to report the death to the coroner but they were too early and were told to return at 11 o'clock. However, they were back again just before 10.00, Mrs Nutt remarking that Mr Withey was very nervous.

From there they made their way to the premises of Simon Howard, an undertaker whose premises were at 18 Gloucester Road, Lawford's Gate. Mrs Nutt was reported to have said either 'We have got a very bad case' or 'We have got a very sad case'. She further explained: 'Mr Withey has got his wife died sudden through the breaking of a blood vessel.' When Mr Howard reached the scene of death and began to measure up the body he noticed a lump on the woman's side and advised Mrs Nutt to 'Mind and point this out or you'll chuck them off the guard'. He was referring here to the inquest jury. Alerted by this turn of events he searched the bed and found a knife among the feathers. It was stained with blood. Mrs Nutt said 'I threw it in there for the sake of the children'.

The inquest was opened the following day at the *George Inn*, Kingsland Road but adjourned until the Thursday so that the post-mortem might take place. On that day such a large crowd assembled that extra police were drafted in to keep order. Mr Page had carried out the post-mortem and was able to testify that he had found a wound in her left side, 6 inches deep which had sliced 2 inches into a lung. The knife which Alfred had spirited away had afterwards fallen into the hands of Mrs Nutt who had returned it to the bedroom where it was found by the police and was described as being 'quite capable of inflicting such a wound'. After the discovery of this weapon John Withey was placed under arrest.

When Frederick was questioned he insisted he had heard no quarrelling in the bedroom that night. He also stated that his mother was undressed when she went to bed whereas his father slept in shirt, waistcoat and trousers. Then Elizabeth Nutt was called. The coroner gave his view that, according to the evidence he had heard, 'the woman evidently wanted to screen someone' and she interjected 'No, no, sir'. She was then closely questioned about her first sight of the body. She insisted she had examined the body but saw no signs of blood anywhere but issuing from the nose and mouth. She laid out the body but one of the other women removed Jane's chemise. She swore she saw no cut in the chemise, no knife on the bed and she did not remove the body from the bed during the laying out process. She afterwards heard about the knife and was present on the Tuesday night when Mrs Crinks advised Alfred to put the knife back where he had found it. Mary Crinks was an old family friend, an acquaintanceship which dated back to the days when the Witheys were still moderately affluent and not drinking to excess. Eventually Mrs Nutt admitted she had gone up and replaced the weapon although she had no recollection of whereabouts she had actually placed it.

Meanwhile another bone of contention was introduced into the proceedings. It had been discovered that the wound in Jane's side had been stuffed with sacking. Mrs Nutt denied all knowledge of this.

Next it was Alice Bartlett's turn to give evidence. She recounted the screams she had heard from the children at about 10.45 on the Monday night. When John Withey opened the door she asked him what the matter was and he said 'I don't know, go up and see'. She described the blood coming from Jane's mouth as 'frothy'. She told how she was joined by Mrs Nutt and that they had endeavoured to administer brandy. She said she watched Mrs Nutt and some of the other women laying out the body and washing her 'as low down as the chest'. She could not recall who had removed the chemise but she fancied she saw some blood on it. She noticed that the dead woman was clutching a piece of bread and the rest of the loaf was on the floor. There was a cup of pickled onions on the bed. The next morning she spotted on her dresser two knives previously having been loaned out and another one – a butcher's knife with bloodstains upon it. She showed it to her neighbours and then, later that day, Alfred came to her house and took that one away again. She averred that she did not know where the knife had been found.

She testified that the Witheys quarrelled occasionally, that they were both in the habit of having beer and that she had seen Withey himself very intoxicated but she had not seen him on the night in question until he opened the door to her late that night. When she first entered the bedroom she was startled at the sight of the children 'almost naked', 'dancing' and bemoaning the fate of their mother.

So, without really committing themselves, the Witheys and their neighbours closed ranks and stuck to their chosen stories. The version they hoped might be believed was that Jane Withey was using the knife to cut up the bread. She dropped the bread, placed the knife in the bed and then, in retrieving the remainder of the loaf, fell back on the blade. Dr Warner of Barton Hill House had assisted with the post-mortem. He shared the opinion that an accident was out of the question. The knife would not have remained in an upright position to cause such a wound. Considerable force had been used to push the knife in.

As the intricacies of the convoluted case were skilfully unravelled by assiduous questioning the behaviour of John Withey himself was carefully examined and the conspiracy of silence among the women in the room that night was breached. Questions hung in the air. Why was the chemise removed and stuffed into a cupboard? Who plugged the wound with sacking? Why were there so many contradictory statements being made?

The knife itself had only been returned to the Withey household on the night before Jane's death. John had left it with a Mr Gibbs some time before after slaughtering a sheep for him. Albert had been sent to retrieve it on the Sunday. Was this significant in any way? What had happened to the children while all these events were taking place? It is to be hoped that one of the kind neighbours took them in.

By this stage the coroner was adamant that the death of Jane Withey was a case of either suicide or murder. There was no possible way the knife could have entered the woman's body accidentally. As far as the suicide theory went he did not think it at all likely that she could have accomplished such a deed without her husband being aware of her actions. Although in a statement he had declared that he was in bed by 7.30 and his wife was out drinking until after eleven the coroner argued this was a contradiction of every other witness involved in the case.

Even the position of the knife was open to question. Mrs Nutt had said she had placed it on the right side of the bed after Alfred had retrieved it but PC Cooper who had had charge of studying the crime scene said it had been found among the feathers in the mattress – a place of concealment which had involved tearing the outer sacking. It was a task which he considered would have taken some time and trouble to complete. It was said that Mrs Nutt hid the knife there 'for the sake of the children'. Having given direction to the jury the coroner then asked them to consider what the charge should be. After an hour the foreman was ready to make an announcement. He said: 'Twelve of the thirteen have come to a decision with which one of us will not agree. After careful and just deliberation, we have come to the conclusion that it is the act of the husband, John Withey.' He also expressed the view, on behalf of the rest of the jury, that Police Constable Cooper was to be praised for his careful, diligent examination of the room and the manner in which he presented the facts relating to the case.

It was deemed the circumstances showed there was a case to answer and John Withey was put on trial for the murder of his wife – with Elizabeth Nutt being charged as an accessory after the fact.

And so the case came to trial. The counsel for the prosecution, Mr Foote, in addressing the jury, said he felt the witnesses 'had not thrown the fullest possible light they might have done on the matter'. He asked the jury to consider the undisputed facts – that the prisoner, the deceased and the four young ones were in the upstairs room by 8 o'clock and that 'somewhere before 10.15 the woman Jane Withey was dead. It was not suggested that there was any other person in the house'. The jury were told that the main question for them to decide was 'how that wound was inflicted – whether self-inflicted suicidally or accidentally; if it were neither of these' they would have no doubt it was murder, and murder by the prisoner Withey. He enlarged upon the knife wound explaining that it had been spoken of as in the side but it was round the curve. The exact location of the entry had been pointed out to them on a plaster model. He drew their attention to the prisoner's conduct and language on the night in question. He submitted that 'while there appeared to be no direct testimony which would substantially establish motive' there did seem to have been some words exchanged with relation to the rent money and they were both 'the worse for liquor'. He then introduced a 'strong painful fact' into the proceedings. While agreeing that several of the witnesses stated the couple lived on good terms – some had even used the word 'affectionate' – he had to make the point that during the previous Christmas period 'the prisoner was seen to throw a knife at his wife with such violence that it buried itself in the door so deep as to require considerable force to draw it out.' And then there was Withey's behaviour on being woken by his son. Why did he fail to seek assistance? The only help came from the neighbours who heard the children's cries of 'murder' penetrating the paper-thin walls. He asked the jury, too, to consider who had drawn the knife from the wound and placed it in a corner where it was found by the boy and to decide who had arranged the bedclothes. If Jane Withey had, indeed, been sitting up in bed eating bread and cheese and had fallen back on the knife – would the clothes have arranged themselves in the manner in which they were found? Also why did Withey say to Mrs Bartlett 'Go up and see what my old woman has done?'. If he thought she had died naturally why would he have employed this turn of phrase?

He then asked them to try to visualise the situation the following morning. Did the prisoners, seeing how their story of the burst blood vessel had been accepted without query, believe that everyone else involved could be similarly gulled? This, said counsel, was the only explantion for the otherwise mad course which both prisoners adopted, continuing with the blood vessel farce and the outright untruth told by Mrs Nutt at the coroner's office that both she and Withey were present at the time of his wife's death. Their subsequent actions – his tissue of lies at the coroner's inquest, stating that his wife had not joined him in the bedroom until 4 hours after he had gone to bed and Mrs Nutt's attempts to hide the bloodstained chemise were the actions of someone assisting in the concealment of a murder.

Mr C Mathews, Withey's brief, called character witnesses – work colleague, William Shipp, who had known him for 30 years, foreman Henry Pullen and William Mountain, super-intendent of the gas works where Withey was employed – all testifiying to his good character. Mr Mountain went so far as to say that if Withey was acquitted he was welcome to return to his old job.

Mr Mathews outlined a likely scenario in the bedroom where the knife wound could have been accidental – the loaf and cut piece falling to the floor, the woman placing the knife by her side on the bed while she bent to retrieve the bread, the knife shifted position as she fell back on the bed and on to the pointed blade.

Mr Metcalfe, who was representing Mrs Nutt, argued that if Withey was found to be innocent then all charges against his client would have to be dropped. He pointed out that she was by no means the only woman in the bedroom and no evidence had come to light showing she was aware that Jane Withey had sustained a knife wound. Also, he asked, why would Mrs Nutt put herself 'within the clutches of the criminal law' by covering up for a man who was neither relative nor close friend?

Mr Justice Hawkins' summing up of this extremely compli-cated case took 3 hours 5 minutes. He carefully examined the events in the bedroom and the disposal of the chemise and the knife and intricately explained the knife wound and its rele-vance. The jury retired to consider their verdict at 7.24 pm and re-entered the court at 8.55. The foreman of the jury then announced that they had unanimously decided Withey was guilty of the murder of his wife, and Nutt guilty of being an accessory after the fact but this verdict was delivered with a strong recommendation to mercy on the grounds of his previous good character and the belief the crime was not premeditated. At this juncture Elizabeth Nutt was removed to the cells and the Clerk of the Assize asked Withey if he had anything to 'urge why sentence should not be passed'. Withey came to the front of the dock with hands clasped above his head and exclaimed:

The Lord knows I am innocent; I am innocent, ask the Lord; I am as innocent as a child; I am innocent, I am. Lord, Lord, look down upon me, I am as innocent as a child just born.

Unmoved, the judge donned his black cap and spoke to the prisoner:

After an anxious consideration, and as patient a hearing as any jury could pay to any case, they had felt it their bounded duty to pronounce you guilty of murder of a very cruel and very treacherous character. They have appended to their verdict a recommendation of mercy, upon grounds which they have stated, and I will take care that their recommendation is forwarded to the Home Secretary; that is all I can do.

The prisoner interceded here and said 'Thank you, my Lord'. In passing sentence the judge said:

The poor woman was helpless sleeping in bed, where at least she may have felt she was safe and under the protection of her husband. You it was, her husband, destroyed her with your cruel hand and for that your crime you must die.

It is reported that the condemned man 'looked most wretched' and before descending the steps leading to the cells 'gave a long, lingering, wistful look round the court.'

Mrs Nutt then was placed in the dock and made a long statement protesting her innocence. She accused PC Cooper of lying in his testimony and informed the court that she was the mother of a family and a grandmother and that it was the first time that she had ever been in custody. She denied to the very end that she had known about the stab wound. Even as she was being sentenced to 5 years' penal servitude she called out 'Oh, my Lord, I am not guilty'.

John Withey was hanged on 11 April 1889 and the four children were orphaned. However, members of the family in the Pennywell Road area took them in and they were able, it seems, to overcome the trauma of that dreadful night and the resulting trial to live normal, worthwhile lives and to marry and have families of their own. A relative of Mrs Nutt living in the Bristol area today recalls, as a child, the name being mentioned in hushed whispers making her wonder what scandal had been committed.

CHAPTER 13

What Lies Beneath
1923

I killed my father.

In 1984 a surveyor from the city's Environmental Health office made a call on an elderly gentleman living in Mendip Road, Bedminster to assess the property. The old chap seemed lonely and anxious to chat in common with many pensioners living alone but the story this man had to tell was a remarkable one. During the time the officer was carrying out his survey he was to hear of startling events that had taken place 60 years before. The old man was called George Cooper and in January 1924 he was a leading figure in what the papers dubbed The Brislington Villa Mystery.

George's father was also called George and together with his wife Louisa (aged 57) had lived in Montrose Avenue, Brislington for about 20 years at that time. Previously they had lived in Bedminster. They were, apparently, a quiet couple who 'kept themselves to themselves'; an unremarkable pair, the wife invariably cheerful and often to be heard singing as she worked around the house. There seems to have been a particular bond between mother and son. In fact they were described as being 'wonderfully devoted', their relationship more like brother and sister. George tended to call her 'Jean' rather than 'Mother'. When George married a girl from Cheddar in 1921 the couple did what many newlyweds did in those days – they shared the parents' house. Within a year their first child, a little boy, was born. In 1923 another child was expected and George's wife went to stay with her parents in the June, planning to return for her confinement in September but, in the event, she remained in Cheddar and her second boy was born there. She and the new baby remained there until 3 weeks before Christmas. Meanwhile, George's mother was looking after the older boy, whom she adored, at Montrose Avenue.

Also resident in the house was a lodger, Aubrey Baker, who had lived there since October 1922 and was an engineer employed by the Bristol Tramways Company.

Both 37-year-old George and his father, who was 59, followed the same trade – that of pattern makers initially at Bartletts of Brislington who were scale makers but when these

The murder scene depicted in a contemporary newspaper. Bristol Central Library Archives

George Cooper and his mother Louisa. Bristol Central Library Archives

works closed down they both found similar employment at Sampson's iron foundry at Malago Road, Bedminster.

So, on the surface, a respectable, hard-working family living in a pleasant suburban villa called Croydon House with French windows leading out to the garden, the windows hung with spotless curtains. A kitchen and scullery jutted out on to the garden where a chicken run had been constructed. Not all was as it seemed, though. George Cooper senior was an inveterate womaniser. He seems to have had a taste for office cleaners. One liaison back in 1918 was with a woman engaged in such work at the tramways office where he was employed at the time. In 1923 he was enjoying a dalliance with a Mrs Goodman, charlady at Sampson's who lived in South Street, Bedminster.

His wife was only too well aware of his philandering and had even confronted Mrs Goodman in her own home at one stage as well as making a complaint about her to Ernest Sampson her employer. This seemed to arise out of a discovery that Mr Cooper had paid for his lady friend to go on a firm's outing.

Nor were his extra-marital affairs Louisa Cooper's only problem. George was later to say that his father had always been an aggressive man who was not averse to subduing Louisa by means of violence and had been known to knock her to the ground and drag her to her feet by her hair. He had also been abusive to George himself when he tried to defend her.

Then, in September 1923, the situation changed. Mr Cooper was no longer seen setting off for work each day and returning when the mood took him. At first Mrs Cooper told neighbours that he had gone away to work but then she had to confess he had run off with a woman. Enquiries at Sampson's as to the situation resulted in George saying he was certain his father would not be returning and it was agreed he could take over the older man's job.

Autumn faded to winter and Christmas approached, one to anticipate with pleasure this year as there would be no arguments to disrupt the peaceful atmosphere. Friends and neighbours were invited round and George played tunes on the piano while everyone gathered round for a sing-song. It was probably the happiest Yuletide the family had ever experienced.

Something was bothering George though, something gnawing at his conscience. By the end of January 1924 he felt he had to confide in someone. The man he chose as his confessor was George Blackburn, his uncle on his mother's side. The brother and sister were close and she came to visit him at least every other week.

George Cooper arrived at his uncle's house in Sandown Road at about 8.30 on the evening of 29 January accompanied by his cousin, George Blackburn junior. He said to his relatives that there had been one or two upsets and his father had gone then he added 'I have put him in a position that he won't come back again'. His auntie asked him to clarify this statement and was told 'We had a row with father, and it had to be him or me'. Again she said 'What do you mean to say, George?' and he finally said 'I killed my father'.

The Blackburns, burdened by this terrible knowledge had been placed in an untenable position. The following day the son decided to ask the advice of a friend of his, another George – George Paul who ran a fried fish shop in Redcliffe Hill. He was an ex-policeman. He knew immediately that his only option was to inform the authorities and the following day, when George Cooper arrived home from work, he was cautioned and

Police officers in charge of the case – Sergeant Carter and Superintendent Ford.
Bristol Central Library Archives

placed under arrest. His mother had already been charged with being an accessory after the fact in the murder of her husband.

Mother and son appeared the following morning in Keynsham Petty Sessional Court. The case for the prosecution was led by Mr A Sefton Cohen and Mr E J Watson defended both prisoners. A brief resumé of their circumstances was given. In the press coverage of the day George Cooper is described as slimly built with light hair and dressed in a grey suit with a waistcoat, although he was not wearing a collar. His mother was crying incessantly.

In the event the pair were charged with murder because she denied the accessory charge immediately, saying 'No, sir, I knew it. I knew what it was for'. After the hearing Louisa was taken to Cardiff Gaol. As she was taken away she called to her son: 'Have I got to leave you? Let me share it. It is my fault. It is my fault.'

Meanwhile, the police were searching the house and soon began paying particular interest to the middle downstairs room where George had been doing some repairs to the flooring after his mother had complained to Henry Poole, the landlord who lived in Chatsworth Road, that some joists needed replacing but 'George would see to it himself'. Mr Poole assumed it was her husband to whom she referred but a few days later the son called at his house with a similar story and was told to purchase some timber and put the trouble right and he would be recompensed. In the end he claimed the 17 shillings spent on wood but refused labour costs and money he had spent on the tar used to seal the ends of the joists. On 10 January 1924 he officially took over the tenancy, saying he had heard nothing from his father.

At last the body of George William Cooper was discovered beneath the boards of the very room where his wife and son had celebrated Christmas with friends and neighbours to the accompaniment of many a well-loved tune on the piano, positioned over his 'grave'. Those present at the soirée dined out on the tale for many years afterwards. An autopsy was ordered and marks on the skull carefully examined. The celebrated Sir Bernard Spilsbury was called in to give his esteemed opinion and the case prepared to go to trial.

The trial itself took place in Wells with a special charabanc hired to take police and witnesses there. The accused said in a clear voice 'I am not guilty'. His mother, who had been bailed, looked strained, nervous and tearful. Mr Emmanuel, for the Crown, opened the proceedings by giving a brief background picture of the family ending with the information that the victim had been last seen by his friend, a man called Simms, on 6 September 1923 after they had spent some time on their allotments, paused for a glass of beer and then bidden each other 'good night' at about 8.00 pm. Cooper was seen walking off in the direction of his home at that time.

The accused then took the stand, describing in detail the quarrel that had taken place that night over 'a woman from Goodhind Street' whom his father had threatened to move into the house after turning out his son. To calm himself he went into the other room and began to pick out a tune on the piano, then suddenly became aware his father had crept into the room armed with a hatchet. A fierce struggle then ensued of which the accused claimed to have little memory except that a black and red mist came down over his eyes. He then came to and found himself lying at right angles to his father who appeared to be dead. When his mother returned later that evening he told her what had happened and the following day buried the body beneath the floorboards in the middle room.

It was then the moment for Mr Emmanuel to discuss the head wounds, of which there were nine. If the jury were satisfied that these blows were rained on the victim by the man in the dock then, in law, that was murder. To reduce it to manslaughter he said 'the onus of proof of justification lay with the prisoner'. There was also some dispute as to whether some of the marks had been made when actually removing the body from its temporary grave but this seemed unlikely in view of the forensic evidence. The skull was produced in court and Mrs Cooper held her handkerchief over her eyes.

None of the witnesses called seemed to have anything good to say about the deceased, describing him as surly, hasty-tempered and averse to any sort of criticism. He openly boasted about his conquests over women, even discussing a particular situation with the lodger, Aubrey Baker, when they were having a pint together one night in the *Holly Bush*. He said 'I am in a ***** fix. I have been getting about with another woman and I think my missus has found out'. Baker was shocked because he liked and admired Louisa Cooper whom he considered to be a good housewife and 'one who attended to her home'. He thought too, that 'young Cooper was a nice, quiet young fellow.'

George Blackburn, Louisa's brother, recalled many times he had seen her sporting a black eye and had threatened Cooper with a good hiding. He said Cooper was a man who preferred throwing things rather than fighting and had been convicted in the past of throwing a brick at a man. He was frequently known to smash up crockery, musical instruments and ornaments in the house and was quite blatant about his extra-marital affairs, even once bringing a woman round to stay the night in the family home and insisted his wife wait on her.

At length the jury retired on the Friday afternoon and it was announced that sentencing would take place on the Saturday.

The night must have been a tense one for both George and his mother, so it must have come as a welcome relief when to expiate his crime he was told he was sentenced to 7 years' penal servitude. It was almost as if everyone had felt he had done a favour by ridding society of such an obnoxious man.

The house in Montrose Avenue still stands although the road has been renamed Montrose Park and the case is still spoken of by older residents who remember the family and the shock of hearing the tale of the degradation and misery suffered by the well-liked Mrs Cooper which finally tipped her son over the edge on the night of 6 September 1923, culminating in one of the most shocking suburban killings that Bristol had ever known.

CHAPTER 14

Decoyed to His Death
1924

He had been strangled with a black necktie and sexually assaulted.

O n Friday 15 December 1924 Mrs Amos decided to do some late night shopping. In the run up to Christmas shops tended to stay open even later than usual to catch as much as possible of the pre-Christmas trade. Her husband, a general labourer working on the railway, had gone off to meet up with his friends for a drink at about 8 o'clock. She left her eldest son, 11-year-old Willie in charge of the two younger boys Gilbert, who was 8 and little Walter, aged 2.

The Amos family lived in Burchill's Cottages, Bath Buildings. The cottages still stand although they have now been converted into a single dwelling and the road itself is now known as Upper Station Road.

At about 10 o'clock Mrs Amos, having finished her shopping, walked up to meet her husband accompanied by her friend

The cottage where the Amos family lived – in the process of being modernised in recent years. Photograph courtesy of Amanda Britton

A present-day picture of the school attended by Gilbert Amos. The author

Mrs Green and the couple returned home together. At about 10.30 she went up to the children's bedroom to check on them and found that Gilbert was missing. She alerted her husband and they woke Willie up to find out what was going on.

Willie said that at about 9 o'clock a man whom he knew by name and sight and whom he had passed on the main road an hour before knocked on the door and told Willie that he had come from their Auntie Lizzie's who wanted Willie to go to her house as she had something for him. Willie explained that he could not go as he had been left in charge of the baby but Gilbert, who was in the process of getting ready for bed, offered to go in his place. He hastily put his boots back on and went off with the caller who Willie recognised as someone who visited his aunt. Aunt Lizzie, Elizabeth Morton, Mrs Amos's sister, lived in Portland Street which runs off Acacia Road, a relatively short distance from Burchill's Cottages. Willie noticed Gilbert stop to tie up his boot lace and being told to 'Hurry up'.

Time passed and Willie began to feel sleepy so decided to take himself off to bed. The next thing he knew was being awoken by his parents demanding to know the whereabouts of Gilbert.

Alarmed, Herbert Amos and his wife left the house to search for their missing boy. Mrs Morton said she had not seen Gilbert or sent any message for either of the boys as she had been out the entire evening, from 6.00 until 9.30. The couple continued to comb the area until, at about 2.00 am, they were told to speak to the police. Herbert Amos was taken to Fishponds police station and there identified the body of his son, Gilbert Caleb Amos. He had been strangled with a black necktie and sexually assaulted.

Meanwhile, in North View, a turning off Hayward Road and very close to Portland Street lived the Bressington family whose son, William, had recently returned to Bristol after working away for some weeks. Late on that Friday night his mother must have heard something relating to him which caused her concern and so she went to find her husband. Charles Bressington, together with a friend, William Britton, who lived in Hayward Road, went in search of his 21-year-old son. They found him on a corner of Soundwell Road near the boot factory. From what he said to them, and the exact words were later disputed, he told his father either 'I have done it, daddy' or 'I have done wrong'. He then led them to Cousins' Field near the railway station, now the site of Frampton Crescent, and took them to a

Staple Hill station. Gilbert Amos's body was found in a nearby field. John Merrett collection

corner where lay a child's body. William Britton walked across to examine it and said 'It is a little girl and the body is cold'. He then hurried to the station and fetched a couple of porters who brought lamps and then a police constable arrived. After handcuffing William Bressington he turned his attention to the child, wrapping it in his own overcoat and attempting artificial respiration but without success. The child was now identified as a little boy. Young Bressington had fallen to the ground. He was pulled to his feet and taken into custody. A Staple Hill resident, Joan Davies, was living in Cossham Villa, Lower Station Road when the murder took place and later recalled that from the back bedroom window could be seen all the comings and goings of the police officers that night. She was not aware at the time that the murdered child was a school-mate, though 2 years older than her, at Soundwell Council School (now Staple Hill Primary). Young Gilbert Amos was described by his grandmother as 'a sturdy, jolly little chap, fair haired, chubby' and with 'skin like alabaster'.

The inquest was held on the Tuesday but the accused was not present. Herbert Amos was there, accompanied by Ensign Albion of the Salvation Army, which was always strong in Staple Hill. Mrs Amos had asked him to be there to support her devastated husband.

The funeral took place on the Thursday and hundreds of people gathered outside the house and along the route to Mangotsfield parish cemetery. The little body was conveyed on a hand bier which had been presented to the parish some years previously by local benefactress, Lady Cave of the well-known family. William Frederick (Willie) was there with his parents and his Uncle Gilbert and grandparents Mr and Mrs Wilfred Amos and another uncle, William Graham. Perhaps sur-prisingly Charles and Wilfred Bressington were also present. *Nearer My God to Thee* and *Abide with Me* were played and Ensign Albion read a passage from the Bible. A large cross of chrysanthemums had been sent from the school and also one from Standard 1, the class he had attended.

In the school, at the time the burial was taking place, the children formed an orderly line all round the perimeter of the playground in silence to pay their respects to their erstwhile playmate.

The inquest was resumed the following day and this time William Bressington was present. When he had been brought before the magistrates earlier in the week he had appeared wild and unkempt with his ginger hair hanging down over his face but on this occasion his hair was brushed back. He sat, trembling, with his head bowed.

Herbert Amos was called first and he confirmed that the tie used in the murder had not belonged to his son. He said that, to the best of his knowledge, he had never known the prisoner nor had he ever been a visitor to his home. He described his movements on the evening in question and then had to identify a small pair of navy blue knickerbockers which he said had belonged to his boy. Asked about a 5-inch slit in them he confirmed it had not been there when the lad left the house in the morning.

Young William Frederick Amos was called next and he described the events of the evening. He identified William Bressington as the person who had called at the house.

It was then Charles Bressington's turn to give evidence and he denied that he had said 'This is the ******* who killed the kiddie'. PC 148, John Hawkins, who was called next insisted these words had been uttered and said he had taken a statement from William Bressington, which he had signed, saying 'Yes, I murdered him. I put a tie round his neck'. Mr Stredwick, who was representing the prisoner objected to this saying it would prejudice his client's position at the trial.

Mr Maurice Barber, surgeon, of High Street, Staple Hill, described the victim's injuries and gave his opinion that the child had been violated when he was either unconscious or dead. He said the accused told him there was a third person present, someone called 'James'.

Edward Gould, the stationmaster, testified that he had heard the prisoner say he had committed the murder 'with a tie round his neck'. He also heard the accused say there was another person present but thought the name mentioned was 'Charlie'.

The jury retired for 10 minutes and then returned a verdict of 'Wilful Murder'.

The case came to trial in February. No women were permitted to serve on the jury, nor were any allowed into court with the exception of the accused's mother and sister. Young men under the age of 21 were also barred from attending.

The trial began on a controversial note as Bressington pleaded 'Guilty'. Mr Justice Roche intervened saying this plea was not usual or convenient in murder cases and a plea of 'Not Guilty' was then entered.

Mr S H Emmanuel led the case for the Crown. He summarised the events which had taken place on the night of 15 December 1924 from the abduction of Gilbert Amos to the grim discovery in Cousins' Field. It was at this juncture the case for insanity for raised and the implications detailed. Reference was made to Bressington's remark to his father when the word 'wrong' was mentioned and two questions which the jury had to ask themselves were: (1) Did he know the nature of his acts? and (2) Did he know they were wrong?

Mr Emmanuel stated that he expected the jury to answer 'yes' to each of the questions. He then went on to say that, when the prisoner was arrested, possessions were found on his person of the sort you would not normally expect a young man to carry – face powder, a powder puff and similar articles which the jury might recognise as being abnormal but being abnormal was not to be insane.

After this Herbert Amos, followed by young William Amos, were questioned and repeated the statements they had made at the inquest. Both were questioned about the cut knickerbockers. Mrs Elizabeth Morton ('Aunt Lizzie') repeated her evidence that she had not authorised the accused to take a message to her nephew and then Charles Bressington was called to the stand. He said that he had encountered his son by Derham's boot factory and been told 'I have done it, daddy. I have done it. I cannot tell you but I will take you to the place and show you'. He then described the finding of the corpse in the field. He told the court that his son had been born on 30 March 1908, one of seven children, five of whom, all girls, had since died. He admitted that his son was 'always very funny from a baby onwards'.

Cross-examined by Mr Weatherly for the defence he said that his grandfather had died, insane, in Keynsham workhouse, his uncle David had died in Gloucester Asylum of acute mania and David's son had also died, in October 1910, in an asylum – Bristol Mental Institution. Another cousin had suffered a similar fate.

He said that his son was always in the habit of wandering off and was frequently being brought home by the police. He had attempted to commit suicide when he was 15 by taking poison and was admitted to Cossham Hospital. In August 1919 he ran away and joined the Berkshire regiment but was discharged later that year because of an injury and 'feeble-mindedness'. He remained at home for a short while then took off again and went to work as a steward. On 16 April 1920 he was brought home by the police who had found him in a fit. Over the next 13 months he was away from home and his family had no idea of his whereabouts but in July 1921 he was arrested and sent to Horfield Gaol under the Borstal system for stealing a key and tools from empty houses. From infancy he had complained of pains in the head and had always been unpredictable, going off without a word to anyone. He had, for many years, carried cosmetics and a piece of broken mirror and his father had seen him dressed as a woman on several occasions.

Mr Britton was then called and testified as to Bressington's admission of guilt at the scene of the crime.

Dr William Cotton, the medical superintendent of Horfield Prison said that the prisoner had been admitted to the gaol on 23 December 1924 and was placed on special observation owing to a suicide attempt. He said the prisoner always appeared perfectly rational and controlled and able to conduct lucid conversations on a daily basis. He had had him under his care previously, in 1921, when he had perceived him to be 'unbalanced' but not insane. He described his condition as being one of dull stupidity; one in which he was capable of foolish and impulsive acts.

Two medical experts were called, both directors of mental institutions and PC Trinder of Gloucestershire County Police, based at Staple Hill who had once found him in the middle of the road, arms and legs flailing and screaming 'They are coming over! They are coming over'. When the constable went to his aid he struggled and attempted to bite the officer.

Dr Phillips of Northwoods Asylum had spoken at length with the prisoner regarding his schooldays, his perversions and the actual crime and found the young man answered in a totally detached manner. He believed the accused to be a mental defective with no concept of right or wrong and felt his family history backed up this opinion.

Dr R Barton White, medical superintendent of the Bristol Mental Institution, said he had interviewed Bressington on 11 February and the prisoner had discussed the crime without emotion. He admitted practising as a sexual pervert and said that he had masqueraded as a girl, adding that hundreds of boys did the same. The doctor's opinion was that he knew he was taking the child's life but did not realise the difference between right and wrong.

The judge then summed up and instructed the jury to consider whether the prisoner was guilty of murder in the ordinary sense or whether, as the defence stated, he was guilty but not mentally responsible for his actions. After a little under an hour the jury returned with a verdict of 'guilty' although they recommended mercy on the grounds of his weak mentality. The judge passed the sentence of death but said 'the recommendation of the jury will be considered in the right quarter'. When he realised the judge was donning the black cap Bressington began to sob loudly and had to be supported as he left the dock.

In the event there was no mercy for William Francis Albert Bressington and he was executed by Albert Pierrepoint on 31 March 1925, the day after his 22nd birthday. Given the fragility of his mental state it seems a rather harsh outcome.

CHAPTER 15

Murder on a May Morning
1935

She spoke to him politely,
wishing him a good morning,
no doubt wondering how best
to deal with the situation.

ater the primary witness reflected that it had been a perfect May morning. The early sun had filtered through the trees, spotlighting the dwellings that had been erected there on the slopes of Hencliffe Wood. The papers were to write about the place as if it were a shanty town. The *Evening Post* stated 'The scene of the drama is a curious backwoods collection of scattered cabins – they can hardly be called houses – in which live a numerous population, most of them eking out a hard existence on the land as smallholders and farm labourers'. The Notts' place was referred to as 'a tiny one-roomed cottage' and the Franklins' home as 'a similar cottage'.

The truth was rather different. The children who grew up there loved the woods and living arrangements were not as basic as the press would lead us to suppose. This was no squalid collection of primitive makeshift shacks but homes of which the residents were proud as witness the names they called these homes – The Nook, Woodbine Cottage, Rose Cottage. The children were clean and tidy and attended the local church school at Hanham. The residents were not 'eking out a living' but were pig farmers, kept large coops of fowls and, in the summer months, Mr and Mrs Dyer had a little shop by the river where they sold cigarettes, sweets, lemonade and cockles to passers-by either strolling along the river path or enjoying an afternoon boating.

Prior to the Enclosure Act of 1827 all of this was common land and many squatters lived here. This was before the Avon was made navigable upstream to Bath with the opening of Hanham Lock in 1727 at a time when Bickley Wood began to be quarried for stone. The Netham Dam was completed in 1805 and the Feeder Canal was opened which meant the river could be used for transportation both up and downstream and it was at this time that extensive quarrying began in both Hencliffe and Conham woods. After the Bitton Enclosure Act came into force the land was parcelled up into various portions and sold to anyone who could prove a right of use. Initially the main landowner was Samuel Whittuck of Hanham Hall although John Couch claimed some of the land. After their death the bulk of Hencliffe Wood became the property of the wealthy Richard Haynes whose family seat was Wick Court. On his death in 1919 all his property, in Bristol and London, was placed in the hands of the Chancery Court and a Bristol firm of solicitors were given the task of disposing of the Bristol estates and Victor Osmond was appointed as the Vendor's Agent. It was then that Hencliffe Wood was sold off at a very low figure with deeds carelessly worded and boundaries indistinctly defined and, with the passing years many families did not bother to uphold their claims. In the 1970s Kingswood Council, as it was then known, acquired much of the land.

There were quite a few families living there by 1935. The Littles, the Salters, the Byes, the Robins and the Osmonds were all near neighbours of the Dyers. Mr Elmore had cultivated a piece of land down by the water's edge where he lived in solitude. The Francoms had begun by raising their family of twelve in a little cottage at the top by the Ploughing Field but moved to a larger place at the top of the wood and Harry Nott moved into the vacant property. When he had first married Gladys Slocombe they had lived up on the Batch but this place had better prospects.

Harry was a quiet man who took a pride in his home, fitting a boiler and oil lamps and building a neat little brick path to the front door. In the fullness of time he replaced the wooden gate with a smart metal one. The path and the gateposts still remain.

Gladys was an Easton girl, from Bean Street, rather pretty with dark hair. She married Harry in her teens and, when this story takes place, they had an 8-year-old son called Dennis.

On that perfect May morning in 1935 it was Mrs Robins who ran down the hillside to where Priscilla (also known as Dolly) Dyer lived. She seized upon Dolly urging her to go and see what was going on up at the Notts'. Dolly had heard shots ring out and raised voices moments before. She was reluctant to go for, as she explained, she had her young baby, Olive, to look after but was persuaded when Mrs Robins said she would stay with the little girl. Dolly's sister, who was staying with them at the time, reassured her and so, somewhat reluctantly, she walked up the path.

Mrs Robins found Arthur Franklin holding the gun. She spoke to him politely, wishing him a good morning, no doubt wondering how best to deal with the situation. 'I want to get that black beast,' he snarled. He was referring to Harry Nott. At that moment Mrs Dyer was unaware that the body of Gladys Nott was lying in some bushes nearby but in view of Franklin's state of mind she called out to a boy to fetch the police. More people were arriving on the scene by this time and Gladys's body was discovered. Meanwhile, Harry Nott was crawling across a neighbouring field to a small hut where a telephone had been installed. Ernest Gregory, from Forest Road, Kingswood, delivering coal to a nearby house, probably the Rawlings' place, saw him and went to his aid. Harry was bleeding profusely from his head and shoulder.

Franklin was sitting quietly in the clearing when Police Sergeant Auger from Hanham police station made the arrest. In the meantime the gun had disappeared. It was not found for 3 hours.

At the time the incident took place Dennis was at school. He attended Hanham Church of England School and that day all the pupils were very excited as they were celebrating the Silver Jubilee of King George VI and Queen Mary and they were all presented with a souvenir beaker. That was to be the only bright spot in the day for Dennis who was hurried round to the Robins' where he spent the night, unaware of the tragedy that had unfolded at his home after he left to walk to school.

Dennis Nott during his army days.
George Elliott collection

The reporters were soon on the scene although the *Evening World* representative complained: 'The (Notts') bungalow is a considerable distance from the main road and is only discovered after some distance of walking along country lanes, clearing two stiles and then proceeding over a field.' Having located the elusive residence he noted that 'the small wooden structure commands a fine view across the woods and the river Avon'.

At 11.25 Inspector Symons arrived on the scene where, and he was later to say in court: 'I saw the body of a woman lying face downwards. I examined the body and found the head had been completely shattered. I formed the opinion that the wound had been received as a result of a gunshot fired at close range.' He then went to the hut where Police Sergeant Auger had

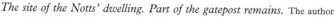

The site of the Notts' dwelling. Part of the gatepost remains. The author

View across to where the Franklin brothers lived. The author

Arthur Franklin under arrest. He said 'I have just seen the body of a woman and shall detain you with feloniously killing and slaying her by shooting her and there may be a further charge of killing a man but you will be informed of full particulars as early as possible'. At this stage the inspector took Gladys to be Franklin's wife.

It was noted that a small wooden shed near the spot where Mrs Nott's body lay had holes in the door and it was ascertained that this was where Harry Nott received his wounds. Another loaded shotgun was found in this shed. Meanwhile the St John's Ambulance crew was summoned and the injured man was taken to Cossham hospital in a critical condition. A police constable remained by his bedside all night.

The water-filled quarry where the subsequent tragedy took place. The author

The whole sorry saga had begun some 18 months earlier when Bessie Gladys Nott had begun a relationship with 40-year-old Arthur Franklin who lived 100 yards away with his brother, Frank, in a two-roomed stone cottage. They were Irish and described as being 'very respectable men'. Arthur was a short, fair, fresh complexioned man. Gladys moved in with the two brothers and her 8-year-old son, Dennis, used to come to the cottage at the weekends to have a bath and have his clothes washed. This arrangement continued until 7 May 1935 when 26-year-old Gladys returned to live with her husband. Two days later she was dead.

It is interesting to speculate on the character of Gladys Nott. It is said she was a quiet woman and neighbours remembered the time before her defection when in the evenings Harry would read the newspaper to her. She must have been very young when she met Harry as she was only 26 when she met her death. Harry was 4 years older. And, indeed, where did they meet? It is known that her maiden name was Slocombe and her father was a dock labourer. At the inquest her mother admitted she had not been in touch with her daughter for 3 years. Harry's family came from Brislington and he had one sister living at home. Regardless of subsequent events no-one seemed in any way judgemental but believed that her head had been turned by Arthur Franklin lavishing gifts upon her. He certainly paid for her to have her hair permed and possibly hennaed as well as the *Evening World* describes her as auburn-haired while neighbours recalled her as having dark hair.

It seems Harry always hoped she would return, possibly for Dennis's sake for, as a Mrs Coles, who lived in Abbot's View, Common Road is quoted as saying, 'Dennis was very much attached to both his parents although they lived apart'.

Mr and Mrs Robins took Dennis in. They were very fond of him as he was friendly with the younger children in the family. The Robins had five children ranging in age from 7 to 18. Mr Robins is quoted as saying 'As long as I have a crust of bread Dennis can have half of it'. He reported that 'Dennis had gone to school this morning. He knows now his mother is dead. Schoolchildren told him about it. I am going to the school today to ask the teachers to see the children do not twit Dennis about the tragedy'.

Meanwhile, Harry Nott lay in Cossham hospital. Surgeons battled to save his left eye but to no avail. However, he managed to rally sufficiently to reassure his son and say 'Hello, Dennis. I am coming home soon'.

Arthur Franklin's initial court appearance at Staple Hill was brief. It was noted that Mr Harris, the clerk of the court, intimated to Franklin that he was eligible for legal aid but the prisoner gave a refusal. He was told he would be given another opportunity later but Franklin said 'You need not go to any trouble. I do not want legal aid,' before being remanded in custody.

The trial itself took place at Gloucester Assizes a few weeks later and was described by the press as 'one of the shortest murder trials in the history of the English Criminal Courts'. The presiding judge was Mr Justice Macnoughton.

Arthur Henry Franklin, referred to as 'a smallholder of Hanham Wood' was addressed by the judge: 'Before you make your plea to the charge against you I have to tell you that you are entitled by law to legal aid. I understand that you have refused legal aid up to now, but I want to tell you before you plead that you can have such aid. Do you desire to have it?' Franklin replied 'I do not wish for legal aid, my lord'. The charge was then read to Franklin who replied in a firm voice 'Guilty, Guilty'.

The judge then placed the traditional black cap upon his head and pronounced: 'You have pleaded guilty to the charge of murder. For that crime there is only one sentence the court can pass upon you and that is death.'

Franklin had shown not the slightest trace of emotion throughout his arrest, initial court appearances and subsequent trial and even now, as the warders led him from the dock he was quite unmoved.

The circumstances leading up to the awful events of 8 May were disclosed to the court as was Franklin's statement regarding his attack on Harry Nott. He had said he intended playing with Mr Nott like a cat with a mouse but he had no more cartridges and was unable to fire the gun. Witnesses at the scene said Franklin had announced he had shot Mrs Nott because she returned to her husband.

In the *Western Daily Press* on 26 June 1935 the public were informed that, whilst in the condemned cell at Gloucester Prison, Franklin had maintained a 'stoical demeanor'. His sole visitor was his brother, Frank, who came to see him on 24 June. The brothers were Roman Catholics and Arthur Franklin received the administrations of the Church from Father Matthew Roche of St Peter's church, Gloucester.

On the 26th, the day of the execution, special precautions were taken by the police to prevent the crowd getting near the prison gates. The hanging was fixed for 8.00 am and at 7.25 Father Roche was admitted to the prison. Just before 8.00 am Mr Sidney Allen, the County Sheriff and the Under-sheriff, Mr

Herbert H Scott arrived together with Mr Edward Graham the prison doctor.

Shortly after 8 o'clock the formal notices of execution were posted outside the gaol by a warder and the crowd surged forward to read the words. The executioner was Thomas W Pierrepoint, assisted by Robert Wilson.

The jurors were compelled to view the body and one, Mr Robert Williams of Quedgley, objected. The prison governor assured Mr Williams that there was nothing to upset him. The coroner insisted it was one of those things that had to be done in important cases as this one was and so Mr Williams had to go with the rest of the jury to do his civil duty. A verdict was recorded that Franklin died in the due execution of the law and his death was instantaneous. The jury donated their fees to the Discharged Prisoners' Aid Society.

So life in the little community began to settle back to some sort of normality. A few months after the events Frank Franklin went to the police and requested the return of his brother's shotgun. As he had in no way been involved in the incident and was of good character, it was judged, the police handed the weapon over.

The part of the woods where the brothers had lived was in one of the long-abandoned stone quarries. Their small, dry-stone cottage stood near to the old working which, over the years, had filled with water to some considerable depth. About 3 feet out into the pool there is a large protruding rock which rises out of the water by a few feet. It was upon this rock that Frank Franklin shot himself using the same gun used in the earlier shootings.

And what of the other survivors, Harry and Dennis? Dennis grew up into a strong, handsome young man. He was called up for National Service in 1945 and served 3 years in the army. After being demobbed he started work with some agricultural contractors, Dennis and Philip Crew Bros, Hencliffe Wood, Hanham Abbots. They assisted with the work on local farms. He began courting a pretty local girl called Betty and they were busy making the final arrangements for their wedding in the late summer of 1948. He was working with the Crew brothers one day, haymaking at a farm, thought to be at the top end of Wick, near to Tog Hill. It was late in the day and work was almost done. Dennis volunteered to take the last bale of hay up the ladder. Whether or not his foot slipped or he simply over-balanced is not known but he fell from the top of the ladder and broke his neck. He was 21 years old.

Harry Nott continued to live in his shack in Hencliffe Wood until the late 1960s when Kingswood Council bought his land and rehoused him at Cadbuy Heath. He later remarried but outlived his second wife. He died at Cadbury Heath in November 1989, aged 84.

CHAPTER 16

Whipping in the Woods in Wellington Hill
1947

... when the borders of dreams meet the edges of reality.

One of the most salacious cases to catch the imagination of Bristol readers was the curious Cornock affair which came to trial during the snow storms of March 1947.

The story had everything to capture the interest of a public jaded by living in the dreary atmosphere of a war-torn city. This was like something out of the movies – a man who loved to be tied up and beaten while dressed as a woman and a disillusioned wife who may, or may not, have fallen prey to the blandishments of a younger man who, rather more conventionally, showered her with flowers and love notes.

Things had reached their culmination on a night in December 1946 when Cecil Cornock drowned in his bath and police officers felt there were suspicious enough circumstances to arrest his wife Ann. There were so many unanswered questions. Why had she waited so long before calling for an ambulance? Why was there a piece of broken pipe lying in the bathroom? What had caused the ligature marks on the man's wrists and ankles? And the injuries to his head? Why had Ann Cornock changed her clothes before enlist-

A newspaper portrait of Mrs Cornock.
Bristol Central Library Archives

The Beehive, *Wellington Hill – the Cornocks' local.* Lewis Wilshire collection

ing medical aid? And what part did her friend Kenneth Bedford play in all this?

The story had begun in 1933 when Rosina Ann Keeling, a nurse living in Bath, had met fresh-faced Cecil George Cornock, an engineer. After a whirlwind courtship they married and set up home in Bath. They were both only 21.

Later, Ann was to say that his cross-dressing and weird demands disgusted her and the only reason she complied was that he was so mean with money that this was the only way of sweetening him up sufficiently to obtain cash for anything beyond the bare necessities. He bought her a sewing machine so that she could make her own clothes. Whether or not she was expected to run up his frocks as well was never revealed. Some might query why, if she hated the life so much, she did not up and leave. Probably because life was extremely difficult for a divorced woman in those days when marriage breakups were regarded, for whatever reason, as shocking. Also, by 1936, they had a son whom they named Maurice. So she stayed and made the best of things. Also, she was later to admit, she felt sorry for him.

At the end of the 1930s they moved up to London but then returned to the West Country in 1941, perhaps because of the horrific aerial bombardment of the capital. They chose Bristol as their new home and chose a rather up-market house in Wellington Hill West. In 1943 Cecil took a job with the Ministry of Aircraft Production which meant he was working away during the week and so Ann had only the weekends with which to contend.

With the ending of the war in 1945 and a return to normality the pressure returned, as far as Ann was concerned. It probably seemed more noticeable after the years of weekday freedom. He became more demanding and enjoyed dressing up and having her accompany him to a nearby wood where she had to tie him to a tree and beat him. Should the weather prove inclement the boiler in the house was used as a whipping post.

In August 1946 Ann met Gilbert Kenneth Bedford in Bath at the funeral of her niece Pauline who had died suddenly while in Bedford's company. The two struck up a friendship and Bedford, whom Ann always called Ken, became a regular visitor to the house in Wellington Hill West. Ken was 10 years her junior, a shy young man who had suffered from severe arthritis as a child and now had to walk with the aid of sticks. Without doubt he felt admiration for the beautiful older woman allied to the sympathy she evoked when she told him of her secret life with Cecil. It was a heady cocktail and she was clearly flattered by his attention. No woman in her situation would surely be able to resist the lure of a younger man offering a shoulder to cry on.

Letters were exchanged which the prosecuting counsel said proved Cecil Cornock was the stumbling block preventing an open alliance between Bedford and Mrs Cornock and he used this argument to paint Ann Cornock as a murderer. The men obviously had very little understanding of feminine thought processes. The whole affair bears an uncanny resemblance to that cause célèbre of the 1920s when Edith Thompson, the original Essex Girl, was hanged in company with her young lover Freddie Bywaters. Freddie killed Edith's husband Percy in a street attack after lying in wait one night when husband and wife returned from an evening 'up West'. Edith's only crime was in encouraging Freddie's belief that one day she would dispose of hubby and marry him. It was obviously 90 per cent fantasy on Edith's part – a bit of drama to pep up her dull existence working in the offices of a millinery warehouse or making loose covers for her semi in Ilford.

The same was probably true of Ann Cornock and dozens of other women in similar positions. The danger lies when the borders of dreams meet the edges of reality. Very likely Ann did bask in the glow of young Ken's adoration and in all probability did look upon it as an escape from the complexities of her rather outré married life but, adaptable as many women are who find themselves in such a situation, she had learned to live with it. The flirtation with Ken was, almost certainly, a panacea to diffuse the underlying tension caused by the darker aspects of her life.

It seems to have been the custom for Ken Bedford to call in the evenings. Ann would be sitting on the sofa knitting or sewing. Ken might browse through the paper, making desultory conversation with Cecil who might, maybe, be engaged in completing a crossword or listening to the wireless. Quite often Cecil would disappear upstairs for a leisurely bath during the course of the evening and later call out for a cup of cocoa to be made which he would take to bed.

On other evenings his tastes ran to other pursuits. On the night of 16 December 1946 he requested Ann put aside her knitting and join him in the breakfast room for 'a game of draughts'. Prior to this request being made Ann had already told Ken this was a double entendre so when she left the room she signalled to him to go into the cupboard under the stairs from which a small window looked out into the breakfast room. Kenneth peered through the tiny gap and saw Cecil dressed in women's clothing, gagged and bound and tied to the electric boiler. Ann was whacking him with a cane. During the procedure her interest and energy flagged and she left him there while she popped off for a cigarette and a chat with Ken.

The following evening when Ken was once again present Cecil requested another session. Ann protested 'but it was only last night', but Cecil was determined. Afterwards she went up and ran his bath and settled back in the lounge with Ken and her knitting. Ken said to her 'It's wicked what he makes you do. It makes me feel quite sick'.

Cecil, exhausted, relaxed in his bath, according to Mrs Cornock's later evidence. Suddenly, she said, it occurred to her that he was late calling down for his cocoa and commented to Bedford 'Cecil has been a long time'. She wondered if, perhaps, he had called down but she had not heard him. She made her way up to the bedroom, calling out as she went but there was no reply. The bathroom door was closed. She walked straight in and saw the water was covering Cecil's head. The water was hot. She grasped his hand and felt for his pulse. It was then, she told the court, she pulled out the bath plug and turned out the pilot light. She lifted up his head and called out for Bedford.

How reliable was this testimony? Giving evidence at her trial, at one stage she had stated that she had let Bedford into the house at 10.30. Later, she had to admit she had lied, because he had asked her to.

So, let us suppose that Bedford came up the stairs to assist her and, between them, they had tried to lift Cornock out of the

The woods where the whippings often took place. Author's collection

Crowds flocked to gain places at the trial of Ann Cornock. Bristol Central Library Archives

bath in order for her to administer artificial respiration. How then could the marks on the head of the deceased be explained? And why had it taken 2 hours for Ann to go out and telephone for an ambulance? And why had she changed her clothes?

At the subsequent trial she was meticulously questioned about every detail of the night in question. Clearly the main point of contention was the delay in seeking medical help. 'Why', asked the prosecution, 'if the man was found dead in his bath at 11 o'clock and there were three people in the house, the prisoner, a cripple who could, however, walk about and a boy of ten, who was mercifully sleeping and apparently did not wake up?' Added to this the house was surrounded by other occupied houses and stood in the middle of a city with medical assistance easily obtainable so why was no help summoned? Mr Roberts, the prosecuting counsel, felt that this crucial 2-hour interval was required 'for those two to decide what they had better do' and that 'evidence might be removed, concealed or suppressed'.

When the ambulance men arrived at 1.07 am they found the body had been moved from the bathroom to a front bedroom on the other side of the landing which was then locked and the key taken downstairs. The five head wounds were noted which Mrs Cornock explained away by saying they had occurred when she and Bedford had been lifting the body from the bath. The doctor, however, was of the opinion that they were most probably caused by five separate and distinct blows inflicted by a flat instrument and, while not sufficient to cause loss of consciousness, could have caused mental confusion. The doctor stated categorically that they had been sustained prior to death.

Attention was also drawn to the ligature marks round the wrists and ankles and marks on the shoulders, elbows and in the small of the back which suggested the scenario of a man struggling against some non-resistant surface, like the sides of a bath, hands tied behind him, struggling, as his legs were being pulled up, to prevent himself drowning.

As Mr Roberts concluded his opening statement he had one more barb to direct at the defendant. He announced:

> *The prisoner on 8 December said it was many years since her husband had had normal relations with her. On 7 February this year, in Cardiff Prison, this woman was found to be 2 months pregnant. Are we not entitled to draw the reasonable conclusion that the love and passion between these two had produced that result?*

Mr J D Casswell KC, led for the defence. He queried the evidence of the head injuries, pointing out that the orthochromatic film used to record the injuries made them appear a shade darker than they would to the naked eye.

PC Buckland who had arrived at the house at 1.25 on the night in question and examined the bathroom was asked what he found. He said there had been no smell of gas or fumes in the room, that the floor appeared to be dry and that there was a denture lying on the right hand side of the wash basin. The flue pipe was not in position, two pieces of it lying on the floor. As he left the room Mrs Cornock had explained to him that the pipe had fallen down when they were getting her husband out of the bath. She had, prior to the fatal night, spoken to the landlord on the matter and he had promised to have it repaired.

She then explained to the constable what had happened, saying that she and Mr Bedford had struggled to get her husband from the bath but he had slipped back and the pair of them had changed places and lifted again which was when Mr Bedford had grabbed the geyser flue pipe to steady himself and it had broken away and fallen on her husband's feet. It was only on the fourth attempt they managed to lift Mr Cornock out of the bath. Between them they then dragged the body along to the front bedroom where she had removed Cecil's denture before beginning artificial respiration. She continued for some time until she began to feel faint and Bedford went to make her a cup of tea. Thus sustained, she returned to the bedroom but decided then that her husband was past human aid and then it was she went to the telephone kiosk to call an ambulance.

At this juncture PC Buckland began to reveal Mrs Cornock's comments to him regarding her husband's sexual preferences but was interrupted by the judge who did not see the necessity for such matters to be discussed but Mr Casswell insisted that the tying-up aspect was of significance so the evidence was ruled as admissible, although not examined in depth at this stage. It was noted that a suitcase full of women's clothing was found which Mrs Cornock said belonged to her husband.

When PC Buckland was asked by Mr Casswell to describe the manner in which Mrs Cornock revealed the details of her husband's secret life, saying 'When she was telling you about these things would it be right to say she was nervous and excited?', the constable replied 'During the whole time I was there she appeared to be nervous and excited'.

Police Sergeant Bernard Graham was examined about his findings, particularly with regard to a toy boat which he had discovered between the bath head and the wall, also the position of the towel. The sergeant said the boat was not concealed in any way and the towel was along the floor at the side of the bath. There had been a suggestion made that the head injuries could have been caused by a flat object such as a toy boat.

Dr Gordon Riach Fells, the Cornocks' family doctor was called and he gave his opinion that death was 'probably due to drowning' and a discussion regarding the time of death and the effects of warm water on *rigor mortis* ensued. Mr Casswell asked him: 'You heard what Mrs Cornock had to say about the tragedy and you left that house without a suspicion that there had been any violence on the man did you not?'

'Yes', said Dr Fells.

'Have you had experience of a man fainting in the bath and dying?'

Again the response was 'Yes'.

The following day Mrs Cornock was questioned regarding the toy boat and the ligature marks on her husband's ankles and wrists. Mr Roberts challenged her story regarding the earlier 'restraint session' in the breakfast room and also took her to task about her seeming inability to be consistent regarding the time element. 'What time do you now say your husband went upstairs to the bath?' he said. 'About 11.00', replied Mrs Cornock. Her explanation on the discrepancy was that 'I was pressed to state a time. I was very undecided ... and they almost forced me to make a rough guess'.

Mr Roberts kept Mrs Cornock under pressure, asking why she had not sent Bedford or her son for help, whether she had destroyed letters from Bedford before going to telephone for an ambulance, whether or not she and Bedford had discussed in detail how best to handle the situation before help was called and whether Cornock's sexual preferences should be mentioned.

She was then asked to demonstrate how she administered the artifical respiration. After this episode Mr Justice Croom-Johnson asked her: 'Do you recollect making your long statement to Superintendent Carter – the one you started making in the early hours of the morning?' Having admitted this she was asked to clarify a few points then he said: 'You then go on to say "It is many years since my husband had normal relations with me," is that true?'

'I meant that he rarely had normal relations', Mrs Cornock replied.

She was asked whether her husband ever fell asleep in the bath and she agreed that he had 'on several occasions' and also that he had complained of 'blackouts'. She explained away letters found beginning 'Dearest Ken' as being something she had done as a joke to convince him she could write a love letter. She insisted her son was there, as well as Bedford, at the time she was composing one particular note. In fact she countered every question with a swift answer, remaining very calm.

The jury, consisting of ten men and two women, took a mere 1 hour 20 minutes to find Ann Cornock 'Not Guilty', to the amazement of many who thought she was destined for the gallows. She made a lasting impression on her defence counsel who wrote of her in his memoirs with her inscrutable, unemotional demeanour. She was later to say that she had resolved, whatever the verdict, that she would meet it like a woman and would be the same Ann Cornock who had always presented a composed front to the world.

And so this attractive, mysterious woman walked from the court and out of the spotlight to spend the rest of her life in obscurity in Bath.

Death of a Good-Time Girl
1951

... CID men swarmed in from all parts of the city ...

The body was found by a young lad early on the morning of 23 September 1951. Nine-year-old Tony Taylor had been asked by his father to fetch the Sunday papers and he dawdled on his way back to Lynton Road via the playing fields. He was idly kicking a stone about as he passed the old air raid shelter and warden's post. The stone rolled towards the entrance. It is clear that Tony did not stop to make a detailed examination of the unexpected scene that confronted him because he ran home and said to his mother: 'There is a little boy hurt in the stone shelter. He's got blood all over his face.'

Mrs Taylor made her way straight to the shelter to see what she could do for the injured 'boy' and was shocked to be confronted with the body of a woman. She ran off to Sheene Road where the nearest phone box was located and dialled 999. She then waited by the kiosk until the police car arrived and took them to where the body lay. By this time it was nearly 9 o'clock. In the 30 minutes that followed CID men swarmed in from all parts of the city and a team was organised under the command of Detective Superintendent Melbourne Phillips. He had three detective inspectors working under him, Jesse Pane, Ivor Godden and J Sargeant.

Peggy Lye pictured in the Evening Post *after the tragedy.* Bristol Central Library Archives

Evening Post *shot of the boy who discovered the body with his mother.* Bristol Central Library Archives

The shelter where the killing occurred. Bristol Central Library Archives

During this half-hour a crowd of several hundred had gathered in the vicinity and most remained there all day despite torrential rain pouring down. Young Tony Taylor, clearly shaken from his experience, was despatched to his grandma's house in Knowle to distract him from the shocking scene he had witnessed.

By 10 o'clock Mr E B Parkes, Director of the Home Office forensic science laboratory in Bristol, arrived on the scene and spent about 45 minutes examining the body. Police photographers took all necessary pictures and tarpaulin sheeting was placed over the shelter. Still the crowd waited even though no further activity took place until Professor J M Webster, the Home Office pathologist arrived from Birmingham to make his initial examination.

By this time the identity of the body was known. A local postman, Brian Stone, made the initial identification. He lived a couple of doors away from the shelter and went to investigate when Mrs Taylor rushed to the scene. The dead woman was 23-year-old Peggy Lye who had lived a short way away in the same road as the lad who found her body. All the locals still referred to her by her maiden name of Marsh although she had been married over 2 years and had a young son, Michael. She and her husband, Ronald, a 28-year-old railway porter, lived with her parents in what must have been a fairly crowded household as her two sisters, Barbara (aged 18) and Christine (11) plus brother Peter (15) were also living there.

Later that day Peggy's mother gave an interview to the *Bristol Evening Post* in which she told the reporter that the last time she had seen her eldest daughter alive was at about 2 o'clock on the Saturday afternoon when she had announced she was off to post a letter and call in on her friend, Violet Poole, who lived in Haldon Close. Mrs Marsh thought that the two pals might decide, as they often did, to go to the cinema. When it got very late the family agreed she must be spending the night at Violet's and decided to bolt the door 'because we heard someone hanging about at the back of the house'. Peggy's father, George, added: 'We didn't know anything had happened until my son George came running into the house this morning.'

George junior lived just round the corner from his parents in Dawlish Road, he and his wife sharing the house with his mother-in-law. He confirmed to the reporter what his father had said explaining:

> *I came round here at 9.45 am to see whether the family knew anything. When I went out this morning a man came down the road and asked me whether I knew Peggy's body had been found in a disused air-raid shelter nearby. That was the first I had heard of it.*

Miss Melinda Herbert was also interviewed and is described as appearing to be 'the last to see Peggy alive', although one would imagine the person most likely to fit that description was the killer. Melinda Herbert was 22 years old and lived in Marksbury Road. She worked as a weigher at Edwards, Ringer and Bigg, tobacco manufacturers, in Redcliffe Street. She had known the murder victim for many years, testifying that 'She was a very friendly girl'.

Evening Post *portraits of Peggy's two friends – Violet Poole and Melinda Herbert.*
Bristol Central Library Archives

Melinda spoke of the circumstances of their meeting:

I had just come from Hotwells on Saturday night after paying some darts money to a club and was waiting for a Bedminster bus on the Centre. The time was about 10.30. Peggy spotted me in the queue and called out 'Hello, Lin'. She was smoking a cigarette and was alone. I stayed in the queue for a time but, as the bus did not come, I walked over to Prince Street. Peggy, in the meantime, had walked past the Hippodrome and up towards Colston Street.

Reporters caught up with Violet Poole on the Monday. This was the Violet that the Marshes had believed had offered Peggy a bed for the night. She said 'I've known Peggy for 15 years. She was a good friend of mine and always had a cheery word for everyone, especially children'. She had encountered Peggy at about 1.15 on the fateful Saturday on her way back from the shops. She continued:

I asked her if she could lend me a cigarette and she gave me two. She told me she was going to meet a man on the Centre between 2 o'clock and 2.15. She had two letters in her hand which she was going to post. She was going to catch a bus at St John's Lane and seemed quite happy. She was wearing a coloured scarf around her head.

The report ended with the bleak statement, 'Mrs Lye has one son, Michael, who will be two on Thursday'.

So what, then, were the events leading up to this tragedy?

The chain of events was set in motion on the preceding Thursday night when Peggy was promenading around the Denmark Street area which had a somewhat dubious reputation at that time. She approached a young man and asked if he would like to go for a walk with her. He was later to admit he took her to be a prostitute but agreed anyway. Peggy was an attractive, lively girl of medium height with dark hair. The young man whose acquaintance she made was called Percy Harold Sanders. He was 19 and had only been in Bristol for a few weeks. He seems to have been a bit of a drifter. He originally hailed from Southall in Middlesex and had joined the army but had been discharged for being 'of a dull mentality'. Returning to Southall he found that he was constantly falling

Sketch map of the murder site. Bristol Central Library Archives

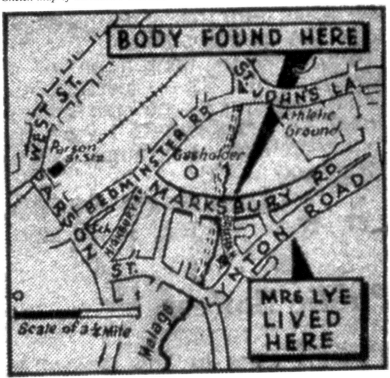

Denmark Street today with Gaunt's House dominating the skyline. It was ill fate that led Peggy Lye to meet Percy Sanders here in September 1951. The author

out with his father who probably criticised him for being dismissed from several jobs because of bad timekeeping. During that summer he had taken himself off to the Isle of Wight where he had worked as a hotel porter then, it seems on a whim, he had handed in his notice and headed for Bristol. As it turned out it was probably the worst move he ever made. He found work in a biscuit factory but on the Tuesday before the fatal weekend he had begun a new job at Hartley's Bakeries in Monk Road, Bishopston.

Peggy seems to have been impressed by his 'London' accent and the two of them wandered off into the night ending up in Victoria Park, Bedminster. He failed to turn up for work on the Friday and he and Peggy spent the morning roaming around the town centre. They encountered a friend of hers in Milk Street, a thoroughfare which connected Newfoundland Street with the Horsefair before the Broadmead shopping centre came into being. Peggy announced she was going to London with her new beau. It is reported that they were 'acting like a courting couple'. Stopping only to make a detour to the bakery to explain why he had not reported for work (he said he had been 'ill'), the pair then made their way to one of Peggy's favourite haunts, a

Denmark Street café, probably *The Holborn*, where they were served by Daphne Alner, a pal of Peggy's. Again, Peggy boasted that she was going to London, 'Aren't I?' she smiled at Percy. She told Daphne she had left her husband and was expecting Percy's baby. She was wearing a ring she had persuaded Percy to give her. If Percy swallowed the story of the pregnancy he must indeed have been of a 'dull mentality' but then, he must have been a bit dazed by the whole scenario. In 36 hours Peggy had virtually taken over his life.

Percy enjoyed a brief respite during the afternoon when he returned to his lodgings for a wash and brush up and Peggy went to her home for a few hours. It is interesting to speculate what explanation she gave for her absence the night before.

It seems when Percy went back to his digs he was accosted by his landlady who demanded the rent he owed. He was clearly not in a position to pay her and was told to 'sling his hook'.

He returned to the Centre at 6 o'clock to meet Peggy who was accompanied by another friend, Violet Steadman who lived in Hotwells Road. The three of them went to the pictures where Percy sat with his arm round Peggy. As they left the cinema Violet heard him say he would buy her a wedding ring. Peggy and Violet then went off home leaving poor Percy to sleep on a bench in the Haymarket which, in those days, was a paved, tree-lined park. No sooner was he settled than he saw a policeman approaching so decided to move on. At 6.30 the following morning he clocked on at work. It being Saturday his shift ended at noon and he hung about until two when he met up with Peggy and Violet once more. Peggy was wearing a mustard three-quarter length coat over a blue skirt. She was bare-legged and wore brown suede lace-up high heeled shoes and a vermillion scarf with white spots. Percy's financial situation had not improved and Peggy was nagging him to pawn his watch. Eventually, at about 5 o'clock, Violet took herself off leaving the young lovers to wander round aimlessly . They finally ended up on Brandon Hill at about 8 o'clock. By this time it had started to rain and Percy must have been feeling the worse for wear. He had slept scarcely at all for the past two nights and had not eaten all day. By 10 o'clock all he wanted to do was lie down and go to sleep. During their walk Peggy returned to the subject of him buying her a wedding ring. Perhaps not in the most harmonious mood they made their way back to Denmark Street.

In September 1951 Gaunt's House was under construction. There was a night watchman's hut on the site and Percy, alone at this point, approached him, asking if he could sleep in the hut. The reason for this request is unclear, being that Peggy and Violet had procured him some new lodgings at 12A St James Parade that very day. Perhaps he could not take up residence until he found a deposit. It must have been at this juncture that Peggy and Melinda were having their chat by the bus stop. When she walked off Peggy must have been meeting up with Percy again to see how he had fared with the watchman.

When she was told he had drawn a blank Peggy said she knew of a cellar in Old Market where they could doss down for the night. She seemed determined to spend the night with him but he said if the police found him it would look bad if he was with a woman. He told her he was really tired and just wanted to lie down and sleep.

Peggy was very persistent though and soon Percy found himself trailing across the Centre in her wake, through Prince Street to Cumberland Road and over the footbridge which spans the river. Peggy was trying to persuade Percy to accompany her to her home but Percy, wisely, was reluctant to involve himself in any sort of domestic dispute with her husband. As they made their way along Dean Lane Percy became aware of someone walking behind them. The man, who was staggering and appeared to be under the influence of drink, overtook them and caught Peggy by the arm, trying to persuade her to go with him. He lurched unsteadily and nearly pulled Peggy over with him. Percy tried to detach himself at this point but Peggy was clutching his arm tightly. An argument ensued. As they made their way towards Sheene Road their dispute attracted attention and bystanders recalled the younger man hanging back and the drunken older man falling down in the road.

Percy's tale of Peggy's reluctance to go with the drunk was denied by other observers who said it looked as though she was pulling him along in the direction of the Malago tip, site of the disused shelter.

The older man, described as being between 50 and 60, rather short, not well-built and wearing a fawn raincoat and a cap, was eventually tracked down by the police at his place of work on 18 October. He had been seen with the couple by a number of witnesses on the night in question. He was, in fact, a 52-year-old labourer from Cavan Walk by the name of Edward Tyrell. He was reluctant to come forward, apparently because he was a married man and had been drinking in a number of different pubs that night, so perhaps he was more scared of his wife than of being indicted in a murder enquiry.

The next reported sighting of Peggy Lye, by an Albert Winter of Marksbury Road, was at around midnight when she was, once again, in the sole company of 'the younger man'. Mr Winter said the man had looked 'dishevelled' and was 'not wearing a collar'. They were arm in arm and she was talking 'quickly' to him. He seemed not to be taking in all she said. He testified that the man was definitely not Tyrell.

Tyrell came to be regarded as an unreliable witness as he changed his story at least once and was suspected of discussing the case with various people. He had attended an identity parade where he failed to pick out the man he had described as wearing a suit 'which appeared to be dark tweed or navy blue'. Then, during his court testimony, suddenly the colour of the suit changed to brown. When Percy Sanders appeared in court he was described as wearing 'a brown suit over a white sailor vest'. During cross-examination Tyrell denied falling down drunk and being hauled to his feet by Peggy and also that he and the girl had been 'lobbing against each other'. He agreed that he did not tell the police that Mrs Lye had said to him 'This is my friend Mr Sanders', nor had he mentioned her grabbing him by the arm.

He said that after he left the couple, telling Sanders he could 'Do as he liked with her', he walked on up Marksbury Road, Dawlish Road and Lynton Road. He then paused at the foot of the steps that led from there to Novers Hill and on to Cavan Walk. He admitted that previously he had said he was in Glyn Vale when he turned back. The reason he gave for returning to the shelter was that he heard a scream which sounded like something 'Between a cat, a child and a woman'. He found Peggy's body lying in the doorway. He felt her arm and concluded she was dead. 'I had the shock of my life. I did nothing else and went straight home.' Did he pause to pick up her purse though? It was not found when her body was removed the following day although it did mysteriously reappear a few days later – in the shelter. He denied all knowledge.

On being questioned about his intentions towards Peggy he bristled with indignation saying 'No, I am a married man with four girls and a boy, and I am proud of them'. He also denied he went back because he wanted to see the woman again rather than because he heard a scream.

At length Percy Harold Sanders was cross-examined. He had made four statements after his arrest, all of them showing variations. He was facing Mr John Maude, KC, the prosecuting counsel and pleaded not guilty to murder.

Percy described his initial meeting with Peggy and the development of their 'relationship' up to the argument in the shelter after which he walked off leaving her unconscious on the shelter floor. Asked why he had not mentioned this incident he replied 'I thought I might get arrested for knocking the girl out unconscious'. He had fully expected her to be waiting for him on the Centre on the Sunday afternoon instead of which he had been faced with Violet Steadman and a group of Peggy's friends telling him Peggy was dead and he should go to the police immediately which is what he had done.

The fact he had not asked Violet and her friends what had caused Peggy's death was called into question but Percy admitted that he did not want to know. He stuck to his story that they had entered the shelter together. He was cold, wet and bone-weary but she was in a livelier frame of mind. His sole desire to find somewhere to curl up and go to sleep seemed to incense her and she became argumentative and aggressive. She grabbed him and pulled him towards her, kneeing him in the 'lower stomach' which caused him to feel faint and giddy. He staggered and grabbed her by the scarf in an attempt to steady himself and they swayed from side to side he said. Medical opinion, though, presented by the prosecution indicated at least three blows to the face delivered by a fist. Percy's version was that when she fell to the floor, banging her face as she did so he took the opportunity to make his escape. The journey back to the centre of town was a total blur and he recalled nothing until waking up on the Sunday morning in the watchman's shed on the Gaunt's House site.

In contrast to Mr Justice Gorman's 3-hour summing up of the case the jury took a mere 35 minutes to find Sanders not guilty of murder and they accompanied their manslaughter verdict, with a recommendation for mercy. He was sentenced to 5 years.

It is quite likely that Percy Sanders is alive today. He must sometimes remember Peggy whom he described as 'a rather dangerous woman' of whom he was 'in one sense' afraid and regret the September night in 1951 when he decided to go for a walk down Denmark Street.

CHAPTER 18

Evil in Easton
1967

She felt her hand which was icy cold ...

The neighbours were concerned. They had not seen 'Mrs Parker' that morning and Easton in the 1960s was still sufficiently community minded for folk to be concerned if there was any variation in anyone's usual routine.

The group of women decided to consult Vi Allen who, like Mrs Parker lived in Britannia Road and knew her rather better than most. It was Vi who popped round with a hot meal for the widow and made sure she was alright.

Everyone still called her Mrs Parker but her name had, for many years now, been Louise Jane Dunne. Time was when she

Britannia Road today. The author

The scene at the time of the murder. Bristol Evening Post

was married to Alderman Teddy Parker, Labour Councillor for St Paul's Ward and a prominent trade union man. He was an ex-docker who had led unemployment marches in the 1930s and was highly respected. He had been tipped as a future Lord Mayor but died during the Second World War before he could be thus honoured.

In the intervening years Louise had married again, this time to John Dunne, a quiet, pleasant Irishman who worked as a night watchman but, in 1960, she had been widowed again. Now, in 1967, aged 74, she had gone downhill. Previously smartly dressed and sociable she had begun to neglect herself and her home. A bad fall the preceding winter had necessitated a hip operation and afterwards the doctor had sent her to 100 Fishponds Road, a grim place which had once served as a workhouse. She hated the regime there and discharged herself before she was well. Since then she took even less interest in food and preferred to get by on a few drams of whisky. Louise took to living in just the downstairs of her house and it was only the efforts of neighbours like Vi Allen and Alice Clarke that ensured she had any nourishing food at all. She had also begun to be increasingly reclusive. Few people were invited into her house and her sharp tongue ensured many kept their distance.

This then was the situation existing on the morning of 28 June 1967. The group of women, friends for many years and members of St Mark's Mothers' Union and the Young Wives, took themselves round to Mrs Dunne's house. They noticed a window slightly open and Vi Allen, who was very nimble, climbed through. The curtains were drawn across and it took a minute or two for her eyes to adjust to the dim light in a room which was crowded with furniture. Vi picked her way gingerly across the room and almost stumbled over the inert form of Louise Dunn lying on the floor. She felt her hand which was icy cold and, peering closer, spotted trickles of dried blood running from her nose, mouth and ears. She went to the front door and announced the sad news to the group of waiting women and someone went to call an ambulance.

Mrs Fortune who lived next door said she thought she had heard a scream in the night, at about 2 o'clock and wondered if that was when Mrs Dunne had been taken ill.

The ambulance arrived and the police were hastily contacted. Vi Allen was told the police would want to question her but they permitted her to go home first and make herself a pot of tea.

Mrs Vi Allen who discovered the body. Bristol Evening News

When they arrived she enquired of them if Mrs Dunne had, as she suspected, died of a brain haemorrhage. They looked surprised and said no, Mrs Dunne had been murdered.

'Didn't you notice the stocking round her neck?' Vi was asked and she admitted she had not in the murk of the room.

There was another, worse shock in store, however. Some photographs were produced with the warning that 'they were not pleasant'. The lisle stocking round the neck was pointed out but there was something else awry. The knickers, pulled down, could only mean one thing. The motivation was sexual. Mrs Dunne had been raped.

In the days and weeks that followed hundreds of statements were taken and every male in the area over the age of 16 had their hands and finger prints taken. Everyone was asked to account for their movements on that day and who they had seen and spoken to. Vi Allen said that coming home from her early morning job she had exchanged a 'good morning' with Mr Yorke from nearby Alpine Road – they passed each other every day as he made his way to work. He was asked to collaborate her statement. The whole district was turned upside down. Everyone was wondering if the killer was someone they knew.

On the day that local papers revealed that the Easton widow had been sexually assaulted the story vied for attention with the news that curvaceous American blonde film star Jayne Mansfield had been killed in a road crash just outside New Orleans. The item was of interest to Bristol readers as the actress had been staying at the Webbington Country Club a couple of months previously and was planning a return. The stark contrast between the two reports added an extra degree of horror to the whole scenario.

Local tramps and down-and-outs were interviewed, patrol cars combed the area and picked up men sleeping rough in the St George and central areas of the city.

One lead given to the police was by a girl who had returned to Easton by taxi on the night of the murder at 2.10 am. As she alighted from the taxi she caught sight of a man, aged about 35, she judged, and about 5 feet 7 inches or 5 feet 8 inches, of medium build and with short hair. He was wearing a three-quarter length brown suedette coat and dark trousers. It struck the girl that he had particularly large hands. When she saw him he was approximately 200 yards away from Britannia Road. An appeal went out to all taxi drivers but no information on the man was ever forthcoming.

What seems to have been Mrs Dunne's sole remaining relative was interviewed, a man called George Robins who lived at Lockleaze. He was her son-in-law. He said he was in touch

Off licence in nearby Bloy Street where Louise Dunne was a regular customer. Mrs Stedman was present when the body was found by Mrs Allen. Lewis Wilshire collection

with her by letter on a monthly basis but had not actually seen her for about a year.

Eventually all enquiries reached a dead end and life in Easton settled back to normality. No-one was ever brought to justice for the murder of Louise Dunne and it is a chilling thought that her killer may still be in the area, his sinister secret safe for ever?

Bibliography

Richard Smith's scrapbook: Bristol Records Office.
Prison Entry Books: Gloucester Records Office.
Transportation Log Books: The National Archives (Kew).
Newspapers: Bristol Central Library
  Bristol Mercury
  Bristol Times and Mirror
  Felix Farley's Bristol Journal
  Bristol Evening Post
  Bristol Evening World
  Western Daily Press.

Index

(1) People

(2) Inns and Eating Houses

(3) Places